SURVIVAL SCRAPBOOK

SHELTER

SCHOCKEN BOOKS • NEW YORK

RITES

———————— Demonstrating, opening,
living, understanding, scratching,
needing, surviving, earthling ————————

————————Using, scrapping, tooling,
clipping, holding, adding, finding,
coloring, cutting, amending,
rearranging, recategorising, feeding-
-back, drawing, filming, printing,
distributing, growing, building,
            growing, building.

———————— Materials and techniques
in here are low-cost, available Britain,
with do-it-yourself technology.————————

ACTION

Various, unpredictable, cloudy, sunny, rainy, wild, moderate, perfect, extreme, simplest, easier, dangerous, lower, greater, fast, suitable, spare, extra, absolute, essential, well-used, slippery, best, available, steepest, sharp, dangerous, very fast, slowest, pale, bright, green, closest, injured, warm, single, tallest, high, exposed, clear, open, wild, bad, true, red, rose, reliable, good, deep, glowing, calm, high, dry, general, settled, rising, faster, falls.

INFORMATION AREA.	INFORMATION UNIT.	(P.A.G.E.)
	forward facing.	back facing.
	TITLE.........................RITES ACTION.......................CLIMATE CONTENTS....................CONTENTS ESSENTIALS..................MAZE.	
	INFLATABLE SUIT...........COLD RAIN..........................FOOTWEAR SPIN OFF....................SLEEPING NO SHELTER.................STRAW BOYS COMMUNICATE.............JOE LA MOOSE ITEM CHECK................CHECKLIST EVERYTHING LIST.........CAVES ONE CAVES TWO................MORE CAVES.	
	SNAIL........................LEAN TO POCKET HOME..............RAINSHELL CAMPING ONE.............CAMPING TWO BENDER TENT..............WIG WAM YURT ONE..................YURT TWO YURT THREE...............TIPI ONE TIPI TWO...................TIPI THREE TIPI FOUR..................TIPI FIVE	
	INFLATABLES...............CUTTING IT OUT BLOWING IT UP............GETTING INTO IT KEEPING IT DOWN........VACUUMATICS PLASTIC FABRICS..........VAN INTRO PROS AND CONS...........WHAT VAN ? WINDOWS...................CONVERSION EXTENSION.................COST CONTEMPORARY STYLE....TRAILER CARAVAN	
	GEODESIC INTRODUCTION...BASIC ONE BASIC TWO...................PEEL ONE STRUT AND JOINT..........PEEL TWO UNIT CONSTRUCTION.......THIN SHEET DOMES. SEALING.....................GREATER CIRCLES PODS.........................FOLDING GEOMETRY PATTERNS...................SERPENT. DOMEBOOK DOMES........BUILD YOUR OWN	

CONTENTS

You can get shelter almost anywhere——
—— wrest it from your surroundings.
the essentials are:

1. <u>Insulation</u>. Particularly from the ground.

2. <u>Windbreak</u>. The stiller the air around you
the slower your body loses its heat. However
it is important to have adequate;

3. <u>Ventilation</u>. Beware of lethal carbon
monoxide poisoning or oxygen defficiency.
Particular care should be taken if cooking
inside.

Few animals can range as adaptably as
man between the extremes of heat, cold
and altitude that this planet can offer.
Aided by new tecnology in clothing and
equipement there is almost no where that
a man cannot go and survive; but built into
the human organism are certain limitations to
the speed at which it can acclimatise to a
new environment.

Most airlines recommend a minimum of
24 hours rest to allow the body to
acclimatise to environmental changes. This is
a minimum; it is often more like a week
before the body adapts to great changes of
climate. Moving from a heated city flat to
the open country the body may need a
month or so to toughen-up. It is best to
prepare the body for any such changes by
introducing them gradually/artificially before
the real change to different conditions
is made.

सूर्य्यबुद्धः

SŪRYA BUDDHA.

CLOTHING PRINCIPLES
(SURVIVAL IN THE COLD)

Clothing is the first line of defence against the cold : if you can, use the layer principle. This means dressing in layers of clothing so that air is trapped between them. Ideal would be: vest, followed by T-shirt, followed by shirt and pullover, and then outer garment, with, say, pyjama trousers under over trousers. But you will have to make the best use of what clothes you have. Take some layers off when you work you cannot afford to collect sweat.

If you have a sleeping bag or can improvise one, take your boots inside with you. If you have spare socks keep them inside your clothes all the time.

The most important part of the body to consider is the head. 20 per cent of the heat lost by the body is lost from the exposed head. Thus it is advisable to wear garments with attached hoods. (Troublesome cold feet may often be warmed by putting a hat on.

Gloves are vital. If you don't have them use anything — say a part of your clothing — to improvise. You should take special care to protect wrists, ears, nose and cheeks.

Watch regularly for signs of frostbite. First there is a loss of sensation in the part affected, followed by numbness and dead white colour. Minor frostbite most commonly affects the ears cheeks or nose-tip. To treat, place a warm hand over the part until it is rewarmed. It should then be kept carefully protected.

CHECKLIST
ESSENTIAL REQUIREMENTS

1. Protection against wind, cold and rain.
2. Adjustable to meet the extremely wide variation of conditions which may be encountered on a single day in Britain.
3. Lightness combined with durability.
4. Ventilated, or of a fabric that breathes, to avoid condensation.

More serious frostbite may be alleviated by placing the feet or hands affected into a warm recess of your own or someone elses body. e.g. armpit or crutch.

In very cold conditions avoid sweating profusely ; move and work steadily ; if your clothes become damp they will lose their insulating qualities.

Additional insulation may be achieved by stuffing newspaper, heather, etc. under your clothes.

"A scouts clothing should be flannel or wool as much as possible because it dries easily. Cotton next to the skin is not good unless you change it directly it gets wet ——— it is so likely to give you a chill, and a scout is no use if he gets laid up."

Baden Powell
Scouting for Boys.

KEEPING RAIN OFF/OUT.

Cagoule, anorak, mackinaw, poncho.

FIG. 26. A CHINESE FARMER WEARING HIS COAT MADE OF RICE-STRAW

A poncho or a cloak is difficult to control in high winds and often get in the way when climbing.

Other garments that are closer fitting and easier to move about in such as the anorak tend to be less ventilated and therefore give condensation problems. A waterproof mackinaw is a compromise between the two and is often the choice of the habitual outdoor man.

It is essential to avoid condensation in very cold weather. In warmer regions condensation is not so troublesome; but you should always have rain protection for the head.

The lightweight nylon cagoule, which is a lightweight and longer anorak, packs into a pocket, keeps out all wind and rain, doubles as an emergency bivouac and weighs only a few ounces. However a lightweight cagoule will not last very long if in continuous usage.

In 3 day rains you will need a pair of waterproof over trousers; with a cagoule or long mackinaw the trousers may be in the form of homemade plastic gaiters which fasten about the knee.

When it rains, the air is filled with humidity to such an extent that it does not have the capacity to absorb any moisture released by the body. At the same time the rain will cool off waterproof clothing to a much stronger degree than would air because it is generally colder than air and because water is a better conductor of heat than air.

This cooling of the garment will give, as a result, the condensation of body moisture on the inside of the garment. This explains why clothing may become slightly damp on the inside under unusual conditions and yet gives to the user full protection on most other occasions.

No. 25.—Helmet, German.

cagoule serving as an emergency bivouac

feet in rucksack

RAIN

FOOT WEAR

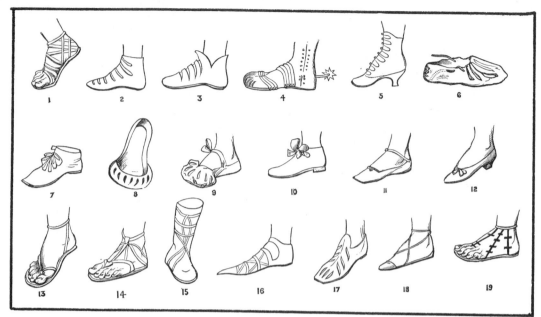

1 2 3 4 5 6
7 8 9 10 11 12
13 14 15 16 17 18 19

Tenderfoot Advice.

"The feet should be kept as dry as possible; if they are allowed to get wet the skin is softened and very soon gets blistered and rubbed raw, where there is a little pressure from the boot.

Of course they get wet from perspiration as well as from outside wet. Therefore to dry this it is necessary to wear good woollen socks. I like shoes better than boots because they let more air in for the feet."

"If your feet always perspire a good deal, it is a useful thing to powder them with a powder made from boric acid, starch and oxide of zinc in equal parts"

"Wash the feet everyday."

Extracts: Baden Powell
'Scouting for Boys'.

Make shoes/sandles from old car tyre treads. These make very tough soles with excellent grip. Moccasins or clogs are also easy to make with simple tools.

lightweight climbing boots.

For city wear shoes are not critical, for general workshoes and for hiking, boots as illustrated below are best.

For Farm work and English countryside in winter, where long walks are not foreseen, wellington rubber boots are necessary. A good type are made for scrambling motorcyclists are very strong, reinforced.

Never save money by buying cheap footwear.

Leather or canvas topped Rubber Boot.

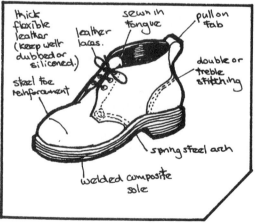

thick flexible leather (keep welt dubbed or siliconed.)

leather laces.

sewn in tongue

pull on tab

double or treble stitching

steel toe reinforcement

spring steel arch

welded composite sole

SPECIALIST SPIN-OFF.

Mountaineering & Hill Walking.

Such people use clothes that are also practical at lower altitudes. For very cold conditions the 'Duvet' climbing jacket is down filled.

However any army type combat jacket and sweater is usually good enough for conditions in the British Isles, although heavier.

Trousers of terylene/ wool mixtures dry quickly after a summer shower and are strong and light. Breeches from whipcord, moleskin or leather are also popular.
Woolen socks and woolen or cotton underwear : rather than nylon.
Wind and water proof over trousers are carried for emergencies.
Other essentials are gloves, a hat and a spare sweater.

British Antarctic Survey.

Good people to consult over winter camping in Britain. However in Polar conditions wet is no problem so they use highly insulated and windproof garments.

Yachting and Seamen

Mostly heavy duty day-glo P.V.C. clothing which is difficult to leap around in and either very garish or overpoweringly 'yachting-type' flavour.

Wigs

Space Man Spin Off.

The N.R.C. Rescue blanket.
Based on a super insulating material that is used in spacecraft the blanket works by reflecting 90% of the persons body heat back to him whilst keeping out rain, wind and snow. It will not crack, mildew or rot and is an effective radar reflector.
Full sized blanket 56" × 84" packs into a small pocket.
Anyone facing the possibility of being stranded in inclement weather should have one.

The Space Sportsmans Blanket.
A full sized blanket that folds to a 8" × 5½" package weighing only 11 oz. A blanket that works on similar principles to the Rescue blanket but the metalised film is backed onto a fabric for more continuous usage.

Motor Cycle Clothing

Motor cyclists wear tough, windproof, showerproof, breathing leathers which you can move comfortably in and work in and are very functional.
Disadvantage : Full leather kit and no bike might confuse communication.

Ex-Army and Jumble Sale.

Best general source of good cheap well designed clothes are the ex-service shops. Cheaper still and with more wiggy possibilities are jumble sale clothes and materials. Sew up exactly what you need for your line of work.

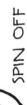
SPIN OFF

SLEEPING BAGS.

When you are lying relaxed and still is when you most need very warm insulating clothing.

The best sleeping bag filling is first quality duck down (not feathers) If you are using the bag in summer only a terylene filling (not kapok.) of at least 38 oz will serve well.

To hold the down insulation nylon is the strongest and lightest, although some people prefer the feel of cotton and it is slightly cheaper. The filling should be in box compartments

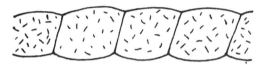

Many cheap sleeping bags have the filling separated by simply sewing the covers together

This method gives serious heat losses at low temperatures. Another method of compartmenting to avoid cold spots is

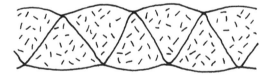

Two simply compartmented bags one inside the other provide 'no cold spots' with the use of a single layer in the summer or the ziping of two together to form a double when another heat source is available

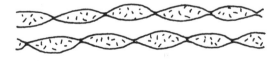

artic type sleeping bag.
weight 4 lb   packed 8" x 15"
be comfortable at 15°F

Where the sleeping bag becomes compressed through the weight of your own body it loses much of its insulating quality. Adequate additional insulation may be obtained with newspapers, heather, fir branch ends, blanket, spare clothes or a hip pad of foam rubber under the sleeping bag. Best of all is the short length inflatable air bed which will double as a chair, placed under the head and torso.

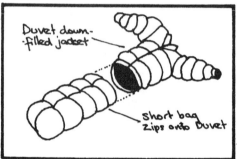

Duvet down-filled jacket

Short bag zips onto Duvet

Why not make your own or even convert old eiderdowns.

Care of Your Bag.

A sleeping bag should be stored, over long periods, loosely rather than rolled up. Down and feather filled bags must be dry cleaned. Synthetic filled bags may be dry cleaned or dip washed.

When in use 'air' your bag daily, turning it inside out or opening the zipper fully.

Note: If a bag has a full length zip it is possible to use it as a bed quilt or zip with another to make a double. The better bags have an inside flap covering the zip so that heat is not lost through it.

NO SHELTER
the case against building.

"It has been suggested that house
building is not a natural act and
is not universal, since for example
the Ona of Tierra del Fuego,
although the climate is almost
artic and the ability to build well
shown by the presence of elaborate
conical huts for ritual purposes,
only windbreaks are used as
dwellings."

Amos Rappaport
'House form and Culture'.

The concept of comfort, which
Rappaport discusses, is culturally
derived. Our ideas of comfort,
comprising central heating, hot
running water etc. might be
meaningless to an American Indian
who might look to very different
things to provide his comforts
ie. conditions in which he might
feel at ease and well cared for.
Being comfortable whilst sleeping
in ditches could be something
other than what you might be
looking for.

A carefully constructed bed of
Broom, which has strange head
clearing properties, should provide
interesting dreams. Angier
suggests a bed of heavily needled
young branches of Spruce or
similar about one foot thick, if
constructed well, provide a sleep-
lulling aromatic ecstasy!

An obvious requirement might be
a good sleeping bag (but tramps
stuff newspapers under their clothes,
which is very effective.) and you
can get down filled mountaineering
jackets called 'Duvets'.

You can build a long fire, brush it
carefully to one side when ready
to retire and then stretch out on the
warm ground.

Waterproof covers are available for
sleeping out. cost weight 2lb.
Might as well use a plastic sack;
condensation problems with both.

Showers don't hurt if you are
toughened to the outdoors and on
rainy nights it is usually possible
to find something to sleep under.
Another thing is to avoid low spots
where cold air collects. It is said
that old campaigners always chose
a place where cows are known to
sleep, to avoid rheumatics.
Guy Underwood, diviner extraord-
-inary found that cows often sleep
over the blind springs of 'aquastats',
which generate beneficial spiral
forces.

THE NOTORIOUS STRAW BOYS: 19 Century Irish terrorists.

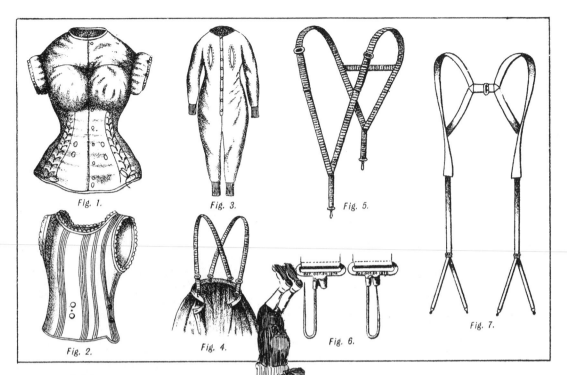

Fig. 1.

Fig. 2.

Fig. 3.

Fig. 4.

Fig. 5.

Fig. 6.

Fig. 7.

UPSIDE
DOWN MAN
COSTUME

BEWARE!

Clothing generally available in shops hasn't improved much for a long time. As with shelter everyday clothing isn't functionally derived from basic physiological needs but is evolved as a part in subtle life games.

Today, in modern society, these games have become so 'subtle' as to be utterly confused. Primitive peoples have clothing forms that are beautiful and symbolically derived and therefore full of meaning to them. The symbolic value of much modern clothing is culturally obsolete.

Specialised groups in modern society, on the other hand, have evolved clothing of a physiological functional and tecnologically sophisticated nature. Functional clothing is often aesthetic without being primarily symbolic, however it soon gets symbolic connotations associated with the myths of that specialisation that it serves.

For example the cowboy —————

" The cowboys personal kit was highly functional, the cut and fashion of his clothes being determined by the needs of his trade which included, the necessity of living with a minimum of equipment and a great deal of mobility. Designed in use, and not to changing fashions, the cowboys kit was the same for generations because it is in complete harmony with its surroundings. Every single article is indispensable."

Escott North
'The Saga of the Cowboy.'

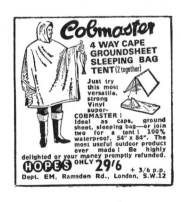

COMMUNICATE

CHECK LISTS

Three day walking expedition (winter time)

<u>basic essentials</u>   <u>emergency items</u>

map   1 pair light windproof trousers
compass   light sweater
whistle   tracksuit
torch (with spare battery   heavy sweater
and bulb)   cagoule, plus 6 x 3 ft. plastic
first aid kit   bag
pocket knife   spare underclothes
matches (dipped in candle wax)   wool shirt
watch   2 pairs wool socks
pencil   1 pair woollen gloves
rucksack   sunglasses (for snow conditions)

<u>camping and personal kit</u>

toilet kit   food (incl. emergency rations)
small flannel   Halazone tablets
tissue paper   eating utensils
trowel   cooking utensils
string   shatter-proof mug
fuel (at least tinder)   tin opener
stove   quality tent (suitable for
down sleeping bag   winter conditions)

<u>Summary of equipment needed for a Large Base Camp</u>

large ridge tents   sewaging chemical
fly sheets   cleaning powder
camp beds or air beds   cooks knives
water cans   chopping boards
buckets   hand bowls
fire extinguishers   iron cooking pots
hurricane lamps   baking dishes
Tilley lamps   tea kettles
folding tables & chairs   frying pans
washing bowls & mirrors   veg. cleaners & peelers
duck boards   puddi ng basins
axes   tea clothes
spades   bowls
picks   plates
chemical toilet (in semi-   cups
rural camp)   knives
toilet tents or hessian & poles   spoons
pits   forks
fuel funnels   salt/pepper pots
fuel containers   milk jugs
rope and cord   cooking stoves

ITEM CHECK

Hudson Bay Company Emergency Kit

waterproof & floating - weight 11 lb. size 12" x 11" x 3½"

Item	Quantity	Purpose
tea bags	28	making of tea
vitamin pills	50	making up for diet deficiency
pilot bread	30 oz.	food
butter	16 oz.	food
strawberry jam	14½ oz.	food
klik	12 oz.	food
condensed milk	14 oz.	food
chocolate bars	10.5 oz.	food
matches	100	lighting of fires
knife	1	multiple purposes
spoon	1	eating, fishbait, scoop or shovel
whistle	1	signaling
double-faced mirror	1	signaling
fishing line	1	fishing, snaring, wick, string
fish hooks	4	fishing, catching birds
snare wire	1 oz.	setting snares & various other uses
candles	2	cooking, light etc.
paper tissues	small amount	multiple purposes
camphor		mosquito bites, cuts, chapped lips

contents maintain one individual normally for one weeks, cutting
exertion to a minimum sustenance can be stretched about four times
as far.

★
Life Support Technology, Inc.

The most sophisticated survival kits and equipment.
Designed for bush pilots and the like.

[Suggested by Alan Kalker]

Catalog

free

from:
Life Support Technology, Inc.
4530 S. E. Roswell St.
Portland, Oregon 97206

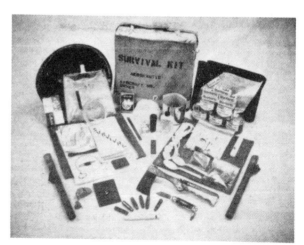

M2/f "Economy" Aeronautic Life Support Unit $89.50

$7.50
Standard Model
10 Ounce

SURVIVAL KIT FOR LIVING OFF THE COUNTRY

Bradford Angiers suggested kit for living off the country

matches in waterproof case	gun & ammunition
compass	sleeping eiderdown
adhesive bandage	tent, tarpaulin or plastic sheet
glasses for sun	flashlight
watch	whistle
maps (+ essential information)	binoculars or telescope
mirror	insect repellant
magnifying glass	short stout candles
sheath knife	fishing line, hooks & sinker
thin blade pocket knife	leads
axe	writing materials
saw blade	canvas bucket
carborundum	canteen
cup & spoon	water purifying tablets
	rope or nylon cord (able to
	support your own weight)

cooking outfit: deep frypan with lid or small nested aluminium pan set.

survival rations: some type of fat ration is most important. Others include chocolate, malted milk tablets, dried whole eggs, dried whole milk, peanut butter, rice, salt + a few pounds of the best emergency food.

toilet kit: 1 small towel/flannel, nail file, soap in waterproof wrapping, toothbrush, dentifrice

repair kit: (Angiers personal) small pair of pointed scissors, 2 rolls of narrow adhesive tape, small pointed tweezers, cutting pliers, 2 short different sized screwdrivers, some nylon line, coil of light snare wire, rawhide lace, tube of all-purpose adhesive (wrapped), rubber patches and rubber cement, small file, various sized safety pins, a few copper rivets, an empty toothpaste tube that with the pitch from a conifer for flux will serve as emergency solder, a small sewing roll with a few coils of thread various needs, wax, a couple of cards with darning wool, a few buttons, a can of gun oil, a few cleaning patches, spare compass, matches in waterproof box, rubber bands, paper clips, copper wire, 3" nails, paper tissues.

medicine kit: (consult your doctor) 1 triangular 40" bandage with 2 safety pins, 6 assorted roller bandages, 6" x 3" sq. gauze compresses, 1 pkt. small adhesive compresses, 1 small bar detergent. 50 or less aspirins, small bottle 2% tincture of iodine, 2 rolls adhesive tape 2" wide, 2 - 4 elastic bandages 4" wide, $\frac{1}{4}$oz. tube of antiseptic anaesthetic eye ointment 1 good fever thermometer, 1 pair small scissors pointed, 1 pair tweezers pointed, 2 curved surgeons needles with ligature & needle holder, oil of clover (or something else for toothache) also instruction book, vitamin deficiency tablets, snake bite kit, kaolin & morphine or similar stomach settler, for isolated regions, upon consultation with your doctor, anaesthetic such as $\frac{1}{4}$ grain morphine sulphate hypo tablets & penicillin.

extra clothing: primarily feet: several pairs of wool socks & a substitute pair of lightweight footwear, large soft silk hanker chief, spare wool shirt. p.s. short air mattress.

survival manual: e.g. How to Stay Alive in the Woods by Bradford Angier, published by Collier MacMillan.

Part or all? of this is packed into either a framed rucksack or onto a packboard.

Skills to be gained before this kit is usable: first, weapon skill, hunting knowledge, wild plant food knowledge, where and what to drink, navigation, general camping & woodsman skills such as making fires or building a bivouac & what trees are what.

Angier on basic clothing: always wool socks, leather boots (composite soles), Levi dungarees (+long underwear) or specially made wool breeches, 2 wool shirts, 1 cotton (many pocketed) mosquitoes peefer blue, strong leather belt, mac. in preference to lighter waterproof anorak because of condensation, tough down filled jacket, leather or wool gloves or mitts.

EVERYTHING LIST

CAVES

There are apparently thousands of caves all over the country. Caving as a sport has a large following but the inhabitability is open to investigation.

The Chislehurst caves were used during the second world war as air raid shelters, when over 15,000 people took refuge in them, many living underground permanently. Gypsies in Scotland lived in caves at the start of this century but I have come across no recent report of troglodites of indiginous cave dwellers in this country. However there are ten million (!) of the Shasni people of N. China living underground according to Rappaport and there are also contemporary cave dwellers in Spain, Turkey, N. Africa, the Canary Islands and Armenia.

CAVE DWELLERS

In Britain there have been cave dwellers in the following places:—

Derbyshire caves at Castleton, Bradwell, Eyam, Matlock, Buxton. Many in Scotland including Wick bay and caves on the Caithness and Sunderland coasts which were inhabited by 'tinkers' in the early part of this century.

Devon, Essex, Kent, Lancashire, Yorkshire, Cornwall, Hertfordshire, Haddingtonshire all have been recorded to have troglodyte inhabitants at one time or another.

Dere holes, which are elaborate inhabited pits/caves are to be found at Doventh wood near Chislehurst, East Tilbury, Crayford, and Little Thurrock.

However in Nottinghamshire, which gets its ancient British name of Tigguocobouc (House of Caves) from its history of troglodyte inhabitation the sanitary officers were only expelling people from their cave homes sixty years ago and the same is true of Kinver in Staffordshire. Shropshire is also reputed to have cave dwellers around this period.

Mr. Wm Stevenson author of 'Bygone Nottinghamshire' relates the storey of a sandman who lived in a cave with his ass. He passed most of his life selling sand about the town of Nottingham. When he 'retired' to a workhouse his cave was explored and was found to be enormous in extent and on two stories. Presumably it was hewn day after day, year after year by the 'sandman'. Its ramifications were so great that a string was needed by the investigators so that they could find their way out again. There is a story of it becoming a lurking place of robbers after the sandmans day.

Caves are still in use in Nottingham but not to my knowledge as dwelling houses.

France is riddled with caves in every department where there is chalk, limestone, sandstone or volcanic tufa. Many were lived in at the turn of the century; whether there are any nowadays I do not know.

Waring Gould in his book 'Cliff Castles and Cave Dwellings of Europe' 1911 gives an interesting account of subterranean homes in vineyards that are valuable enough to need walls around them. The stones for these walls are dug from a quarry which forms a pit accessible in only one place. Chambers are then cut into the quarry walls under the vineyard and windows and doors fitted. A chimney is made by boring upwards and then building around the opening a block of masonry from which the smoke issues.

CLIFF DWELLING ON THE SIDE OF THE CAÑON OF THE CHELLY, A BRANCH OF THE SAN JUAN.

CAVES TWO

The Hermit at his Morning Devotions.   From Goldsmith and Parnell's Poems.

Cave in Ness Cliff occupied by Humphrey Kynaston the outlaw and his horse. 1491 — 1534.

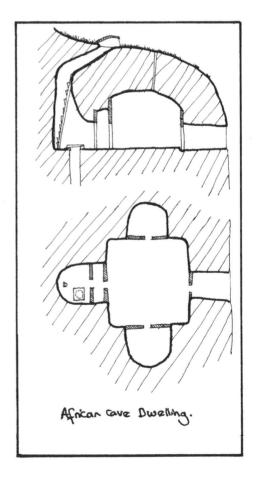

African Cave Dwelling.

Fig. 18.

"Unlike the snail we carry our homes within us." John Cage.

SIMPLE LEAN TO
Cold Weather Shelter

→

thatched with evergreen boughs

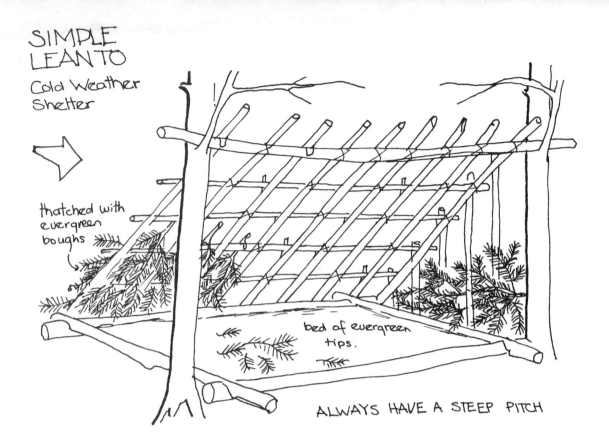

bed of evergreen tips.

ALWAYS HAVE A STEEP PITCH

Slant the light poles from the ridge pole about 8 foot back so a small party can sleep with their heads to a long low fire. The lower ends of the poles can be sharpened and rammed into the ground or held down with rocks. Spacing them about 6" apart. Hold the horizontal sticks in place by weaving and lashing. Openings in the resulting lattice should be roughly 6" square. Now collect a pile of balsam, hemlock or spruce tips and, starting from the bottom thatch the roof with a thick layer. Make a bed inside with more tips aromatic needles, dry leaves, grass, heather etc.

Note the open front of such a dwelling should, of course face away from the prevailing wind.

A rectangle of thin light plastic (say 7'x 9') kept in a pocket will enable such a shelter to be made water proof as well as warm.
A bank of green logs or earth behind the fire will reflect heat into the dwelling. Other thatching materials such as brushwood, straw, grass, reeds, birch bark might be used to tile the roof.
Using these principles larger dwellings may be made for more permanent habitation.
tools — knife, hatchet or saw, ball of twine, sheet of plastic.

LEAN TO

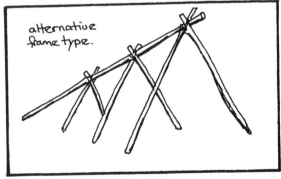

alternative frame type.

THE FORMULA FOR A EMERGENCY SHELTER IS SIMPLE:
WHERE YOU ARE, WITH WHAT YOU HAVE, RIGHT NOW!

HOME IN YOUR POCKET

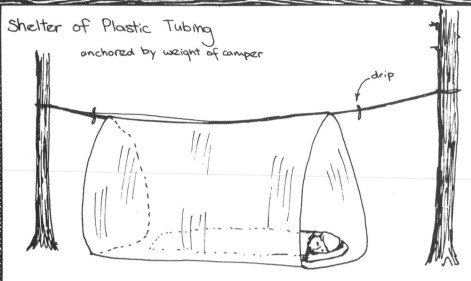

Shelter of Plastic Tubing
anchored by weight of camper

drip

ITEMS

1. 8'x 8' thin PVC sheet
   (polythene is cheaper but doesnt wear so well.)
2. ball of stout twine or 50 ft of nylon cord
3. sheath knife or axe
4. cooking. receptacle

5. air mattress
6. solid fuel stove } "luxuries"
7. flashlight

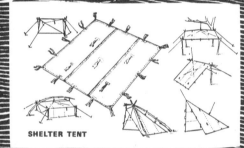

SHELTER TENT

FOLD

round pebble

BEAN STRINGING

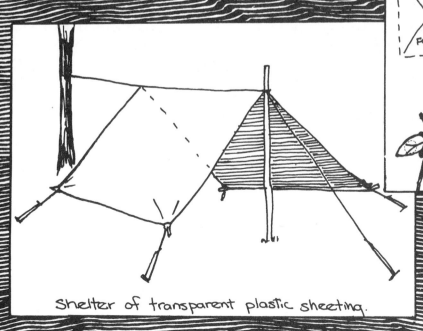

Shelter of transparent plastic sheeting.

POCKET HOME

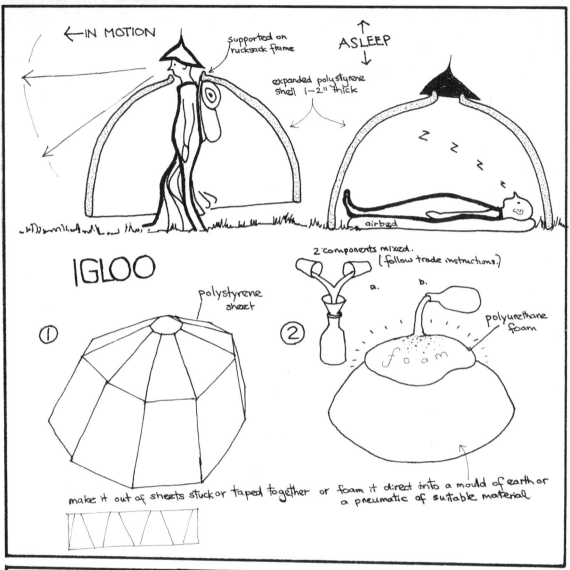

← IN MOTION

ASLEEP

supported on rucksack frame

expanded polystyrene shell 1–2" thick

Z Z Z Z

airbed

IGLOO

① polystyrene sheet

② 2 components mixed. (follow trade instructions.)

a. b.

foam

polyurethane foam

make it out of sheets stuck or taped together or foam it direct into a mould of earth or a pneumatic of suitable material

P.V.C. or Polythene tube

hoops or spiral plastic extrusion, wire or split cane

worn in rain →

RAINSHELL

packed (in transit)

CAMPING TENTS

The main types of tent on the market are one pole, ridge pole or A frame. The ridge tents are the most popular, the single pole the lightest and the A frame the best and most stable.

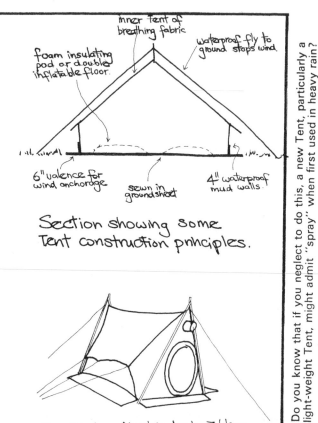

inner tent of breathing fabric

waterproof fly to ground stops wind.

foam insulating pad or double inflatable floor.

6" valence for wind anchorage

sewn in groundsheet

4" waterproof mud walls.

Section showing some Tent construction principles.

single pole 2 man tent 4' high 6'6" long weighs 9 lb 3 oz with pole and flysheet.

The Blacks 'Tinker' tent. A streamlined 2 man all weather tent 9'6" long, 5' wide at main pole and 5' high, With flysheet it weighs 11 lb 14oz

There is a trend toward all nylon fabric as this is very light weight. A tent of 7lb is possible with poles and sewn in groundsheet and flysheet. Minimum size for a one man tent should be about 3' 6" high x 6' 6" x 2' 6".

Poles : These are best of a light weight aluminium alloy. eg. Duralumin.

Guys: Terylene or nylon guys are better than hemp as they do not shrink.

Pegs. Steel skewer type for least bulk but may also cut wooden pegs on site.

Note.

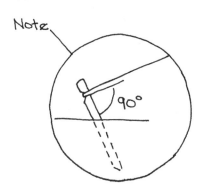

90°

The Blacks Mountain tent 7' long 4' wide 4' in height. weighs 17lb with flysheet.

3 man mountain tent 8' long 4'9"wide 4' high with flysheet it weights 20lbs. A very sturdy tent.

A flysheet is most important for any inclement weather cold or wet and will increase the comfort of a tent considerably. The best type of flysheet is made of nylon or terylene waterproofed with polyurethane. It should come down to the ground so that wind cannot whip beneath it.

Grommet making.

TENTS of OTHER SHAPES.

The above illustration shows the shape of one of the most sophisticated types of small tent. The hooped poles are of fibreglass and hold the lightweight nylon fabric in tension resulting in fewer guys being needed. The hoop shape is aerodynamically stable and doesn't flap in the wind. It provides more head room than an A frame type and it is claimed that the thermodynamics of the internal shape give good ventilation with minimal heat loss. A single wall tent 10' x 5' x 4' high weighs as little as 2½ lbs with poles!

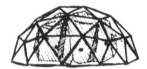

A very stable type of guy-less frame, especially for larger tents, is the geodesic.

A U.S.A. tent called Amazing Tetrahedron. weighs only 5 lbs.

The 'Igloo' tent. The pressure ribs are blown up like bicycle tyres to form a pneumatic frame. rather heavy.

Guyed masts consist of one-dimensional central elements subjected to compression and surrounded on all sides by one- or two-dimensional tension-loaded elements. They thus form three-dimensional systems most suitable for mobile structures.

CAMPING TWO

THE BENDER TENT

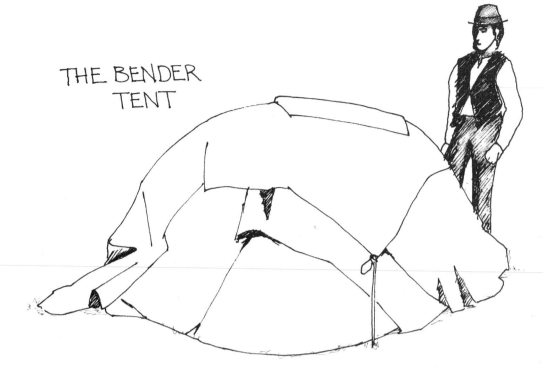

The Bender tent is a domical frame of willow or other flexible branches depending on what is locally available. The framing is tied up with string and can be quite complex with enough room for a whole family. This framework is then covered with layers of felt, canvas tarpaulin and other available scraps of material until the thickness necessary to give the required insulation is reached. So with a thick covering it can be a warm dwelling. The Bender Tent was used by Gypsies in the south of England until the early 60's and is still being used by Travellers in Scotland. It may be erected quickly with materials at hand paticularly by a person with some experience who can improvise forms other than the simple dome shown here.

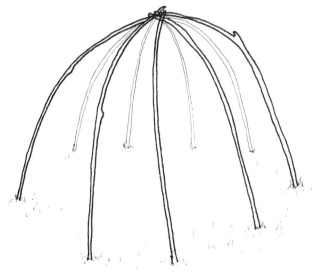

Basic framework, this would then be made into a strong lattice with the addition of cross pieces.

WIGWAM

The covering may be birchbark, rush mats, canvas, felt, leaves, plastic sacks............
Type of covering may be changed in accordance with weather conditions.
The closer the lattice is made, the smaller the pieces of covering may be that are fixed to the frame with large thorns or metal tacks

Bunks made of lashed poles are often built into the inside walls of the wigwam.

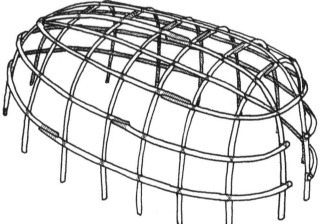

Any kind of green sapling may be used.
If the bark is removed the frame will last longer.
The butt ends are set into the ground about one foot.
Any suitable cord may be used to bind the poles together.

Wigwams of 60' long 20' wide and 8' high were built by the Menomini Indians 50 years ago. The upright poles for these were about 3" thick at the butt ends.

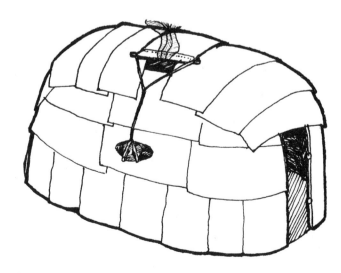

WIG WAM

PHOTOGRAPHY BY JORGEN DISCH, COURTESY OF NATIONAL GEOGRAPHIC MAGAZINE

YURT or GER

ONE

THREE

TIPI ONE

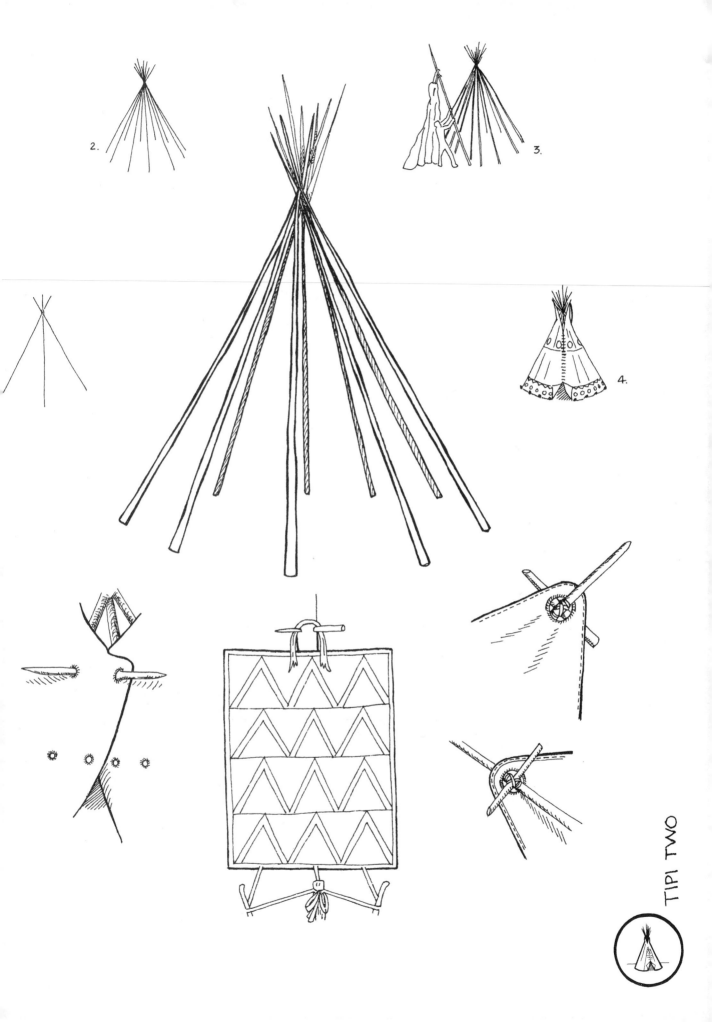

2.

3.

4.

TIPI TWO

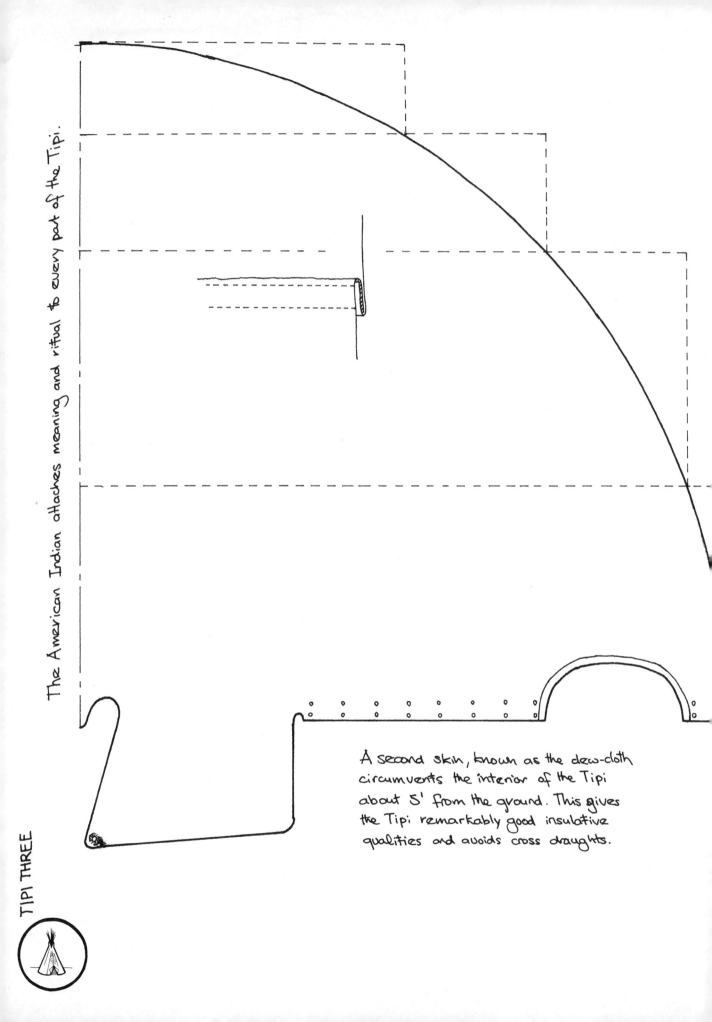

The American Indian attaches meaning and ritual to every part of the Tipi.

A second skin, known as the dew-cloth circumvents the interior of the Tipi about 5' from the ground. This gives the Tipi remarkably good insulative qualities and avoids cross draughts.

TIPI THREE

TIPI FOUR

TIPI FIVE

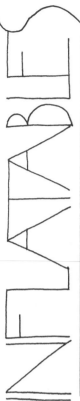

This dome erected by students at Portsmouth in 1967 to publicise the poverty of the built environment, is made from 200 sq. yds of polythene cut into triangles on a geo- -desic pattern and joined with 1200 ft. of P.V.C. sellotape. It is 20 ft diameter, 15 ft high with a clear floor space of 250 sq. ft.

A slight increase in the internal pressure, which sup- -ports the structure, is main- -tained by a small electric fan which provides one complete air change every 4 minutes.

Dismantled the pod can be carried by one person and can be erected in less than ten minutes.

The dome was destroyed on its 3rd. day up by high winds (it was repairable) It would have been more stable as a semi sphere rather than 3/4 sphere. Anchoring was by sandbags.

INFLATABLE

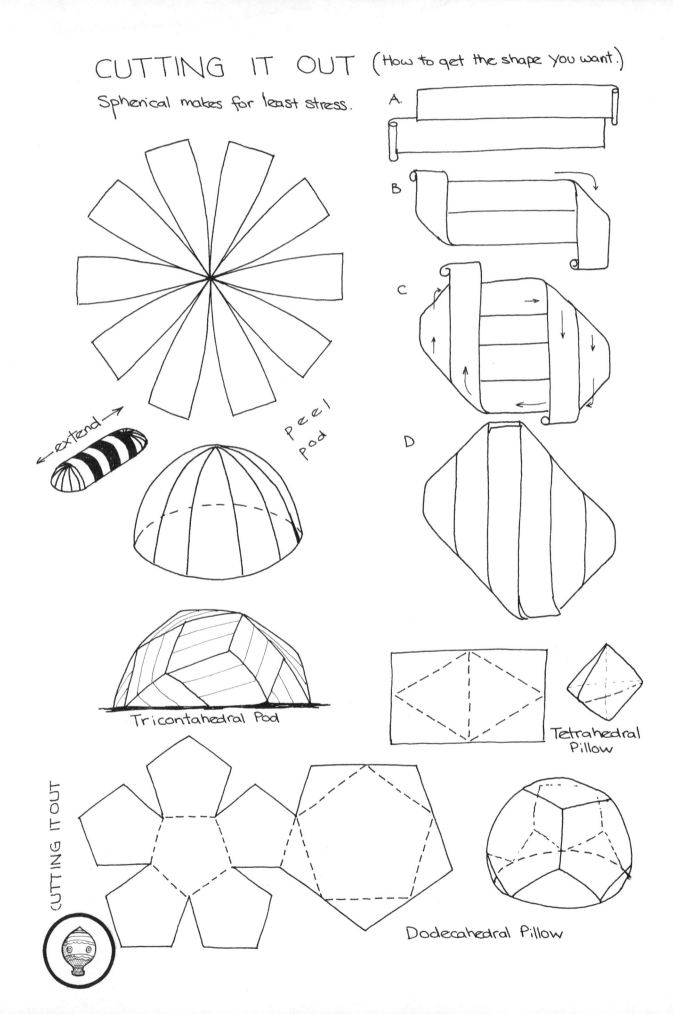

CUTTING IT OUT (How to get the shape you want.)

Spherical makes for least stress.

A.

B.

C.

D.

←extend→

Peel Pod

Tricontahedral Pod

Tetrahedral Pillow

Dodecahedral Pillow

BLOWING IT UP (blowers.)

Blower Size Guide. (warm weather)

A 10' diameter pod needs a fan delivering						1000 C.F.M.
20'-30'	"	"	"	"	"	2000 — 5000 CFM
30'—100'	"	"	"	"	"	(5000 — 15000) x 2. C.F.M.

This guide is only approximate; the fans indicated should be able to deal with fairly blustery wind conditions, average warm day and a lot of entering and leaving. They would also inflate a dome in a reasonable time.

The size of the fan depends on,———

1. The pressure necessary to maintain the shape of the building in expected maximum wind gusts.

2. The size (volume) of the inflatable and its shape. (aerodynamic and low lying shapes will need less pressure to keep them stable.

3. Solar energy heat input expected and the cooling needed. i.e. through air current required.

4. How fast do you want to inflate.

BLOWER UNITS
CAPACITY APPROX. 250 C.F.M. FREE AIR

Secondhand in working order similar to illustration. Controlls Co. Shaded Pole Motor 230 volts A.C. internally mounted and direct coupled to aluminium impeller size 5¾" x 7⅛" diameter and mounted inside pressed steel housing overall size 12" x 8½" x 10½" with double inlet 5½" diameter and single flange all round drilled in each corner for fixing. outlet size 6½" x 5½" with ⅛" mounting

This type of centrifugal fan, available in larger sizes, is the type used in air conditioning systems.

At public events or with large or dwelt in air houses it is essential to have a second blower and stand by power supply for safety.

This type of blower can be hired and gives between 900 — 10,000 C.F.M. and 27,000 — 100,000 Btu/h. heat output from a mobile propane source.

24" diameter ¼ h.p. direct drive fan surplus — suitable for conversion

Offices converting to air conditioning chuck out old direct cooling fans which are good; or you can simply make your own fan. Safety check : strong guard most important or some innocent will have their hand taken off.

If you are using a generator check for overload protection ——— variable power generators will burn out old motors very quickly.

Buying used motors/fans ——— don't if the motor heats up after test running it for 15 minutes.

Home Made Manometer

Check out your pressure difference, wind fluctuations, door losses etc. with this simple to make manometer.

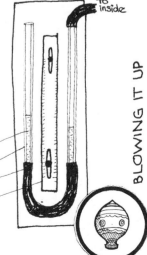

to inside

water
glass tube open to outside
rubber tube
moveable scale.

GETTING INTO IT (enter answers)

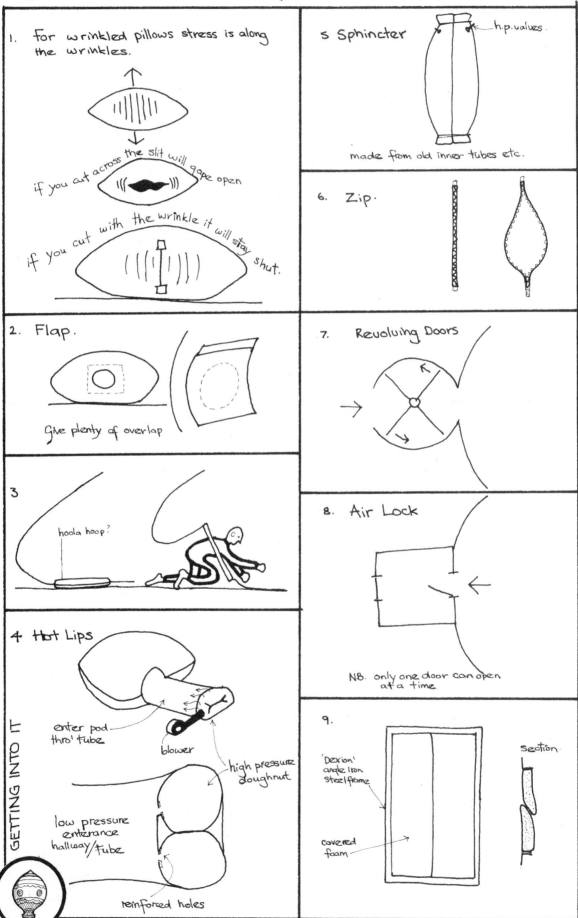

1. For wrinkled pillows stress is along the wrinkles.

if you cut across the slit will gape open

if you cut with the wrinkle it will stay shut.

2. Flap.

Give plenty of overlap

3

hoola hoop?

4 Hot Lips

enter pod thro' tube

blower

high pressure doughnut

low pressure enterance hallway/tube

reinforced holes

GETTING INTO IT

5 Sphincter

h.p. valves.

made from old inner tubes etc.

6. Zip.

7. Revoluing Doors

8. Air Lock

NB. only one door can open at a time

9.

'Dexion' angle Iron steel frame

covered foam

section

KEEPING IT DOWN (anchorage/foundations)

1/ Buried Edge

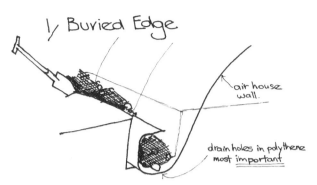

air house wall.

drain holes in polythene most important

Very simple cheap inflatable. Large greenhouses are done this way. Disadvantage — slow to dismantle & needs suitable heavy soil.

2/ Water Tube

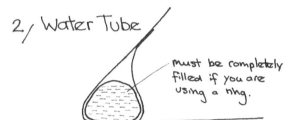

Must be completely filled if you are using a ring.

Note: sand bags, cable, pipe or anything else heavy, may be substituted for water tube. advantage of water — availability.

4/ Nets and Guys.

A cheap anchorage is by up and over guys to available mass such as cars, street lamps, parking meters, trees etc.

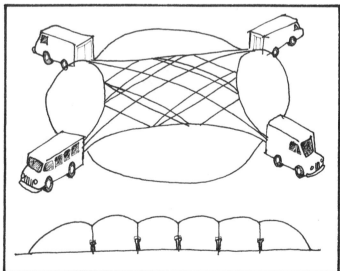

Density of net/guys depends on the strength/thickness used ie. the thinner the material the closer the net.

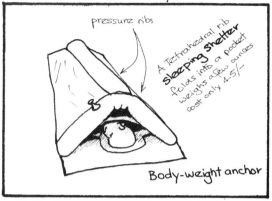

pressure ribs

A Tetrahedral rib **sleeping shelter** folds into a pocket weighs a few ounces cost only 4-5/-

Body-weight anchor

Ground Anchors.

A.　　B.

C.

5/

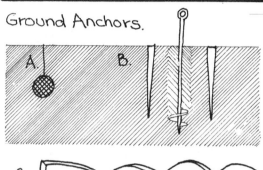

reinforced airhouse wall

continuous fabric flap seal

continuous fabric flap weighted with sand bags.

steel anchor pins at 3' centres. (screwed pins to be used in soft ground.)

6/

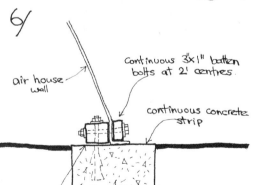

air house wall

Continuous 3"x1" batten bolts at 2' centres.

continuous concrete strip

continuous 3"x4" timber rag bolted at 3' centres. or may be pinned direct to ground ground.

VACUUMATIC

In Vacuumatic structures the body is a flexible envelope partialy filled with particles of material. When the envelope is evacuated, the external air pressure squeezes the bag and close packs the particles within making the whole rigid.

Unevacuated the bag is completely flexible but as it is evacuated the particles come into closer contact and the body becomes increasingly rigid. While it is semi rigid the body may be 'moulded' to some extent.

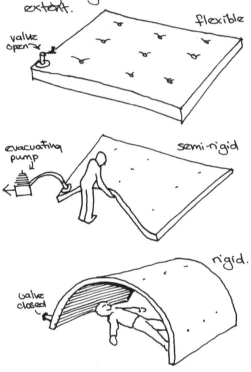

flexible

valve open

evacuating pump

semi-rigid

rigid.

valve closed

This structure of polythene sheet and polystyrene beads is very light and has excellent insulation values.

Joints in the bag are inherently stronger than pneumatics since the skin stresses tend to pull the vacuumatic joints together.

Vacuumatic components may be clipped together to form complete buildings or combined with other materials.

Vacuumatics can be made from a variety of skin materials and many different fillings. The skin may be preformed although there are difficulties in keeping the filling evenly distributed.

The nature of the filling will effect how many forms the body can be made to take. Polystyrene beads are good as they will pack into almost any shape. However when shaping is of less importance many other fillings may be used. Structural units have been made at the Architectural Association using tincans, pine needles, twigs.....

The character of a man/family/group may be read from their refuse.

The daily rubbish is a partial history.

Non compostable rubbish might be put in bags and evacuated. Thus the house might be extended by evacuating garbage.

If the bags were transparent then the walls would be historical records.

Monthly rituals as a new section is added.

Carefully selection of packagings with a view to it being part of the wall next month.

Cornflakes sell best with wallpaper designs on the packet.

Old clothes, gadgets, games, furniture, broken toys, books, (this scrapbook), would all take their part in the wall.

A sense of time and place and

the social embarassment of a large house.

PLASTIC FABRICS
Materials — joining — safety — reinforcement

Plain Polythene is best for amateur builders because of its cheapness and the ease with which it may be joined. The thickness generally used is 4-6 mil. (6 mil = .004")

It may be obtained very cheaply from a builders merchant or off cuts may be begged. Under optimum cond-itions of minimum sun and wind and rough'n'tumble the material will last about one year.

Colour Usually clear or black (building polythene) which are not good for heat build up. White is much better and is obtainable, as are other colours. A good arrangement for a pillow inflatable is to have ½ clear and ½ white. It is turned clear side up on a cool day and white side up on a hot day. Projections made onto white or frosted polythene are very good. If you order a large quantity you can have whatever color you fancy.

Joining 1. Heat Sealing. Use a heavy model electric soldering iron

press down
move along

tracing paper will 'bubble' as weld is made.

tracing paper
polyethylene
cardboard.

here it is.

2 Taping. Simpler but tape is not cheap or easy to get. Use at least 2" wide waterproof tape. P.V.C. 'pipe wrapping' is best. Avoid wrinkles when taping as they collect water and will eventually destroy the bond.

3. Sewing. Best with plasticised fabrics or reinforced plastics is to weld and sew or tape and sew. You'll probably need the heavier industrial type machine. Some of these do 2 or 3 rows of stitching at once.

Poly Vinyl Chloride P.V.C. is a lot softer and a lot tougher than poly-thene. It lasts 2-5 years and will withstand lower temperatures than polythene (30° below.)

It can be taped but not heat welded. You need a high frequency machine to weld vinyl. (hire.) It also costs many times the price of polythene.

fire P.V.C. can be fire proof but polyethylene (polythene) is not.

Reinforcements Commercial Air houses are often made in nylon or terylene proofed with polyurethane or P.V.C. Sheet P.V.C. may be reinforced with a nylon or terylene net. Polythene may also be reinforced in this way. (and also with wire mesh.)

Guide

1. Polythene 500 gauge 4p sq. yd. available in rolls 4'—24' wide.

2. Polythene reinforced with 3/4" nylon mesh. 600 gauge rolls 4'2" wide @ 15p sq. yd.

3. 500 gauge metal reinforced polythene with 1" galvanised wire mesh rolls 4' or 6' wide @ 40p sq. yd.

4. flexible P.V.C. 30p sq. yd. in large sheets or in rolls.

5. P.V.C. reinforced with rayon mesh 40p sq. yd.

NB. Reinforced Polythene is not so easy to tape as it is not smooth.

Polyester film ('MELINEX') mirror silvered with a vacuum deposit of Aluminium. strong until pierced, then it splits and falls apart. Also will not take continuous folding. Cost about 25p per sq. yd. Makes amazing crackling magical mirror infinity domes!

Clara's vardo was planned in the tradition gypsy way, with bed at
the back, wall shelves, an iron stove burning wood scraps standing
on the left-hand side of the door. All was clean and orderly. To
sleep everyone, the bed is drawn out to fill the floor space. Chil-
dren sleep on the bedding compartment underneath. Everyone in this
Hampshire family consisted of nine persons plus two jackdaws in a
wicker cage. Bunches of dried herbs dangled within.

"Kesey gave the word and the pranksters set about it one afternoon.
They started painting it and wiring it up for sound: and cutting a
hole in the roof: and fixing up the top of the bus so you could sit
up there in the open air and play music, even a set of drums and electric guitars and electric bass and so forth, or just ride. Sandy
went to work on the wiring and rigging up a system which they could
broadcast from inside the bus with tapes or over microphones, and it
would blast outside over powerful speakers on top of the bus. There
were also microphones outside that would pick up sounds along the
road and broadcast them inside the bus. There was also a sound system
inside the bus so you would broadcast to one another over the roar of
the engine and the road. You could also broadcast over a tape mechanism so that you said something then heard your own voice a second
later and could rap to that if you wanted to."

                              tomwolfeelectriccoolaidacidtest

"He saw a house in the suburbs slide gently out of its place, and glide majestically along the road, a lady at one of the windows kissing her hand to someone in another house as she passed."

The Mummy
A tale of the 22nd century
John Laudon 1827.

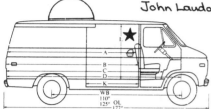

nomad section:

When I first began living on wheels about a year ago it had few of the problems I had expected. It is very easy for me to wash regularly, cook easily, sleep well, crap well and perform all the essential life rituals with almost as much ease as if I were living in a normal house.

Mobile Advantages

1/ Sleep practically anywhere. If your van is reasonably anonymous, as mine is, with no side windows (but a large skylight!) it is possible to live in the centre of london without much trouble. Parking is a matter of common sense and experience —— as few as possible passers-by, nearby public toilets, trees to look up into, commercial vans not uncommon etc.

2/ Diet becomes more interesting as I buy from farms, small-holders and houses in different regions. Spent some days in the countryside gathering.

3/ Meeting many people: ideas/exchange/action moves very fast. Tend to sleep in a variety of homes — no one can believe I'm as comfortable in the van.

4/ Carry people and things. Able to move small crowds, parties, small buildings, firewood etc.

5/ I can do what I want with my own limited space: much preferable to being limited in what you can do in someone elses larger space (i.e. rented flat.)

6/ Many ways of getting money are available when you have a largish vehicle — selling, distributing, casual carrying, using cooker, heater, sounds, generator. X ————

—— You are able to take jobs in isolated places and have a place to live

7/ Free energy. — read in bed by roadlight coming through the skylight.

8/ Self sufficiency unit/capsule * at places where people are screwed under commercial pressures e.g. at pop festivals.

9/ Extensions from the van make any space you want possible once you are parked in a place where it is not necessary to be surreptitious.

Mobile Disadvantages

1/ Mechanics. Unless you are a lover of outdoor mechanics; stand-up-in size vans do not fit into most garages so repairs have to be done on the roadside unless you can afford costly garage maintenance. Even new vehicles need regular attention and care; vans that sell for less than $500 need this regular care to a greater degree. Should be prepared to spent several hours a week working on/under it.

2/ Permanent Address. A good idea when travelling is to arrange to have a permanent address as endless difficulties are caused by 'no fixed abode'. Another legal point is that you are not 'living' in the van but just sleeping tonight, on holiday, for a short time etc, as 'living' in vans is unpopular with the Law.

3/ Few visitors especially if regularly moving (an advantage?)

4/ Increased wind noise. (I find this pleasant now)

5/ Having to go out to get water, baths, crap etc. is usually not a disadvantage if you are well organised.

PROs AND CONS.

Choosing a Vehicle

Small motors such as minivans and
2CV eastate wagons are alright for
crashing overnight or during a rainy
weekend but for continuous living
their size is severly limiting. However
if you have a minimum of possessions
it can be done, most activities being
done outside. I have lived for 3
weeks in a minivan; but a friend
lived for about 3 months (with his
girlfriend) in a 2CV eastate in
London. Remarkably he was doing a
regular job at the time.

However for most purposes of living
permanently from a van, a 20-30 cwt
is about the smallest type that will give
reasonable room. One of the first things
to discover is whether or not you
mind not being able to stand erect.
Extending roofs make Domobile vans head
height but are not really suitable for
towns or winter.

A 35 cwt. van, as often used by bakers
our laundrymen, is about the biggest
van that is still easy to manoeuvre,
park in a meter space, drive under
low bridges, change tyres, drive
through gateways and give reasonable
fuel consumption. (200 cu.in. deisel
gives 20 mpg.) Larger motors up
to pantechnicans are ideal if you
don't intend to move very often
or if a group of people want to live
together. Unbelievable insides can
be built into such vehicles. Special-
-body vans are worth looking out for,
as many of the internal fittings may
be adapted or used as they are—
— especially insulation. This is
the most important physical
requirement. Heating will be
difficult and condensation a
problem without insulation.

WHAT VAN ?

Choosing a Vehicle.

Windows or skylights are simple to fit so light is not essential although a translucent roof is nice (increased condensation tho') Take time to ensure you get something you really want that is mechanically and structurally sound. If you have not much experience of motors yourself get someone with more knowledge to come with you. A second opinion is valuable in any case.

Commercial vehicles become available because they have become uneconomical and unreliable. However a van with 50,000 miles left in it would only last a typical industrial firm six months but it might last you four or five years! A van that belonged to a large concern is more likely to have been serviced regularly.

Sources of Vans — Exchange & Mart, Local Government Auctions/tendering, Ambulance service and Post office tendering, Private Auctions, directly approaching firms, and dealers (often the worst way.)

Rooflights don't come into all this and have certain advantages.— Good light, access to the roof, best position for adjustable ventilation.

A 35 cwt van (this is the weight the van can be loaded with its actual weight might be about 2½ tons.) may be taxed for the same as a car and insured for about the same as a car of similar engine capacity. It is a good idea to take into account a range of good tools when deciding how much to spend.

Cutting Holes in Vans
Can either be power drilled out and then hand filed or started with the drill or axe and then use tin snips. Practice with the snips on a derelict car first. If you are an axeman it can all be done with the axe.

FRICTION ADJUSTER

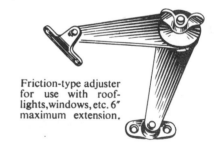

Friction-type adjuster for use with rooflights, windows, etc. 6" maximum extension.

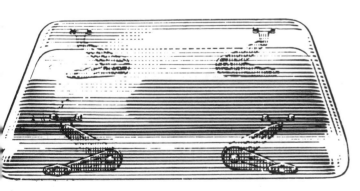

NOTE: All perspex rooflights are supplied **undrilled** and **less** fittings. Perspex is drilled simply and safely with an ordinary twist drill.
Where replacements are required quickly it is advisable to state a second choice of colour.

The roof lights should be at least 3" larger than aperture to allow adequate weather protection.

Converting a Van.

When buying furniture for the van it is wise to get things that will give the greatest flexibility in use. For instance an inflatable quilt type mattress is easily backpacked when you want to get off the road. An ex navy hammock packs up into nowhere - an ideal extra 'bed' for visitors. Four inches of polyether foam is about the most comfortable mattress and it is possible to roll it up.
Useful materials for making removeable bed platforms and storage space quickly are bolt up angle iron like 'Dexion' and ½" chipboard.

The most important thing about van fittings is they must be able to be fixed or held down in some way. Particular care should be taken with inflamable liquids and bottled gas such as the petrol primus or 'calor' gas. Details of cooking and heating devices are given in the energy section page. Appliances should be 'spill proof' as well as secured — this means it is not advisable to used unpressurised kerosene equipment.
Lighting by electricity is best from a flourescent strip light which will use less energy from your battery than a tungsten light. For long periods of immobility, really anything more than 3-4 days, you will need an ancillary battery and special charging mechanism; or if you could do with some heat as well, a pressurised kerosene lamp such as the Tilley lamp is very good. A useful strip light is the hand-held type on a long wire which enables repairs at night to be done with much greater ease than with a torch.

Water Storage (and disposal.)
Most conveniently kept in a 5 gallon polythene or metal 'jerrycan'. The water holder itself may have a tap or a small hand pump which supplies water to a bowl. Drainage through a hole drilled in the floor with a large funnel jammed into it or directly from a bowl. If you are staying for some time in one place waste water should be caught in a bucket and discarded into a suitable drain.

Sanitation. Permanent W.C. enclosures are impractical in all but the larger vans — but a folding screen and separate ventilation are quite easy to arrange.

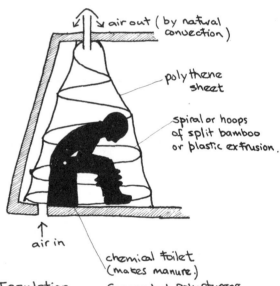

air out (by natural convection)

polythene sheet

spiral or hoops of split bamboo or plastic extrusion.

air in

chemical toilet (makes manure.)

Insulation —— Expanded polystyrene sheet is the best material (an alternative is corrugated cardboard). You will need at least 1" thick for winter quality insulation. However a great reduction in condensation will be obtained if the walls are lined with thin polystyrene sheet. It is possible to stick this thin polystyrene (bought in rolls from a wallpaper shop.) to curved forms; so to get 1" of insulation over curved forms it may be built up from this thin sheet. The polystyrene may be covered with vinyl faced paper or painted hardboard. If it is not to be covered it should be a self extinguishing polystyrene which is slightly more expensive.

Life Support Vessel ?

There are many ways to
e x t e n d   o u t . . . . .
The weight of the vehicle
can be the basis for many
types of extension, acting as
an anchor for their stability.

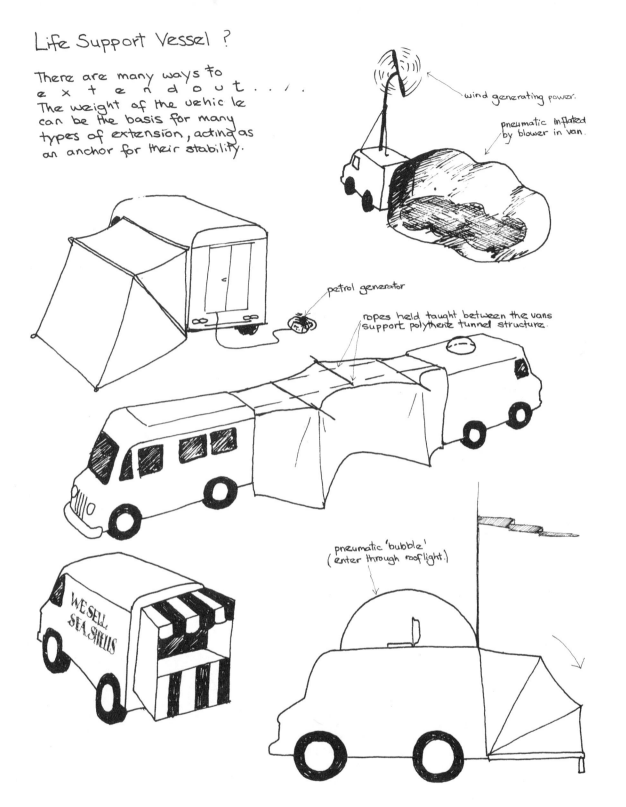

wind generating power.

pneumatic inflated
by blower in van.

petrol generator

ropes held taught between the vans
support polythene tunnel structure.

WE SELL
SEA SHELLS

pneumatic 'bubble'
(enter through rooflight.)

Selling ice creams, pop corn, balloons, telling stories, punch and Judy, flags, theatre for men who dig holes in the road, sense out pneumatics kept up by generators, windmills, disco, searchlights, play at busmen, video makes the spontaneous and disinteg- rated mobile school, barrel organ,

caravan origionally meant a group of traders bonded together for safety bookshop, library, screen print, film shows, macrofood, circuits and bases, routes and havens, cultivation of deserts, poster poems, sewing machine makes clothes, power drill makes workshop, dark room, information micro film file, inflatable boats, buskers & trampoline.

EXTENSION

RUNNING DETAILS

VEHICLE.......Bedford 1965 220 cu. in diesel engine 4 wheel 35cwt.
            Hawson body insulated and lined

1. The van as bought: Poor body work.....needed fibreglass
                       & respray. Good runner, new tyres, good
                       batteries etc.

2. Conversion costs: fibreglass & respray. Did the work our-
                       selves, bought cheap spraygun, used poly-
                       urethane yacht enamel, which was very good
                       paint.
                       Inside there were: 2 polyether foam mat-
                       tresses, covers for these, $\frac{1}{2}$" chip-
                       board for bed shelf, 2 burner cooker
                       & gas bottle deposit, food hamper
                       water container, pots & pans,
                       skylight

3. Reconditioned injectors.......a critical part of the diesel
   engine. I had this done in a garage.

4. Three punctures - one very bad. (above average)

5. Oil & filters, brake fluid, antifreeze.
   note: diesel engines need different oil to petrol engines.

6. New parts: nearside handbrake cylinder, differential needle
               bearing and diff. seal, side window, tail pipe &
               hanger, side light lenses, engine mounting studs
               handbrake cable.   (very reasonable)

7. Tools: quality adjustable spanner, screwdriver, pliers,
          moles etc.   (not enough!)

8. FUEL.....derv. 7,600 miles at 20 m.p.g.

9. Insurance third party, fire & theft.

note: I did all the servicing myself.

By looking at this, you can see where you could make savings or spend
more. For instance: an average of 146 miles a week, is rushing about
rather a lot, periods of rest (or work) off the road, will bring down
overall costs considerably.

P.S. I also bought: a gas heater with gas bottle, a Tilley
kerosene pressure lamp, portable flourescent light, fire
extinguisher, covent garden grass floor.

COST

"Indian arrangements were far to casual for our eyes (my entry shall point north because my god is the bear and the entry of his den points northward and he may remember me.) yet the vocabulary of shapes was so intrinsically rich that a fine architect would find rewarding life long occupation in mastering it."

"The nomad way of life is fully capable of developing an orderly expression of its own and the idea that it is essentially predatory is based on prejudice."

Douglas Haskel   Pencil Points June 1943

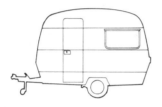

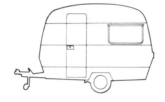

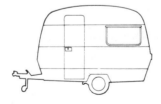

CONTEMPORARY STYLE

TRAILER-CARAVANS

The standard modern caravan is usually very well designed so that the small dimensions are in fact a large space. Normally drab, ugly and similar, they can however be picked up a decade or so old and parked in a friends garden.
However, check your local Bye-Laws here, as some councils will not allow a caravan to be kept in the front garden.

Possible advantage of getting a workmans style hut, is that you could park in the street in very obvious places, and be taken for workmen (?) camouflage.

Getting permanent sites for caravans apart from existing houses is difficult, or expensive, and the existing sites are often visually barren.

Guardian — The most popular of all.

Super Guardian — to give even more room, more luxury than the Guardian.

European — 23 ft. — The six berth holiday home

Fairground folk have successfully developed the trailer caravan most. They have organised summer and winter sites and the vans of the more successful are extraordinarily lavish, with cut glass, bone china, fine mirrors and more recently heavy chrome flashing. Other aesthetically pleasing jobs are the old type wheeled wooden workmans huts, with wood burning stoves, quaint chimney, and shutters over the windows.

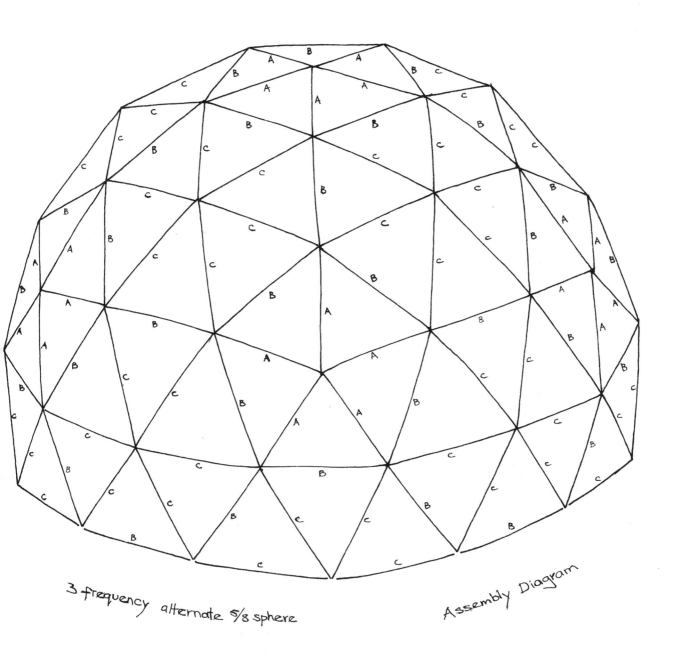

3 frequency alternate 5/8 sphere

Assembly Diagram

'GEODESIC' DOMES

This is an <u>icosahedron</u> the regular solid from which most geodesic domes are derived.

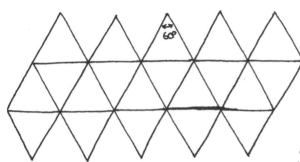

This is the layout for a cardboard model of an icosahedron.

You can make small structures using the icosahedron but it is usually convenient to subdivide the triangles of the icosahedron for larger structures.

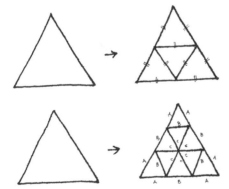

The simple division is called 2 frequency; the other is called 3 frequency. The 3 frequency division of the icosahedron is a good frequency for 24—39' domes.

BASIC ONE.

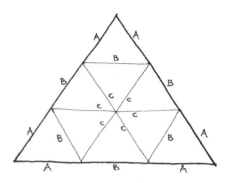

a chord factor is a pure number, which when multiplied by a radius gives a strut length. There are three different strut lengths A, B, C. in the 3 frequency subdivision shown above.

chord factors

A — .3486

B — .4035

C — .4124

> In a sphere there are 60 A struts 90 B struts 120 C struts

chord factor X desired radius = = length of strut.

If you make a model of a three frequency sphere you will discover that it may be cut off, to form a dome, in 3 ways, depending on its orientation in space

MODELS
In making geometrically derived structures <u>models are essential</u>.
Two main types.
1. Strut models from swab sticks, matches, cocktail sticks. Dip both ends of a bunch of sticks into some contact adhesive such as Bostik and allow to dry 10—15 minutes. Separate sticks and construct.
2. membrane or card models. Use a compass to make templates then use the template to draw out as many components as you need. Tape components together on the 'inside'

DOME MISCELLANY

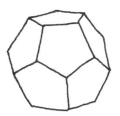

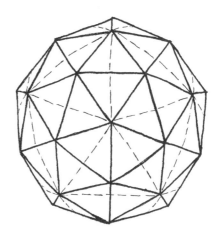

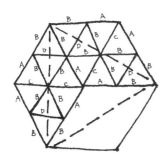

DODECAHEDRON

to stabilise this regular solid you must put 5 spokes into the centre of each pentagon.

every triacon breakdown has : 20 identical triangular faces from the icosahedron, 30 identical diamonds from the triacontahedron, 12 identical pentagons from the dodecahedron.

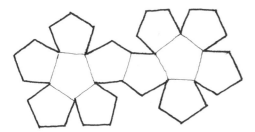

a 4 frequency breakdown of the icosahedron.

chord factor

A ——	.3134
B ——	.3361
C ——	.3628
D ——	.3894 ✳

In a sphere there are 60 A struts
180 B struts
60 C struts
60 D struts

dotted line is the face of the icosahedron. You need 30 diamonds to make a sphere.
This is another useful breakdown for home sized domes.
This type of breakdown, where the face of the icosa. is not outlined, is called 'Triacon'. Were it is outlined as in the previous 3 frequency breakdown it is called 'alternate'.

✳ color code or you'll be confused!

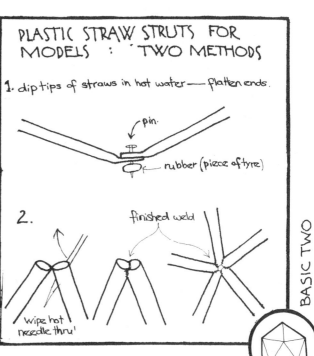

PLASTIC STRAW STRUTS FOR MODELS : 'TWO METHODS

1. dip tips of straws in hot water — flatten ends.

pin.

rubber (piece of tyre)

2.

finished weld

wipe hot needle thru'

BASIC TWO

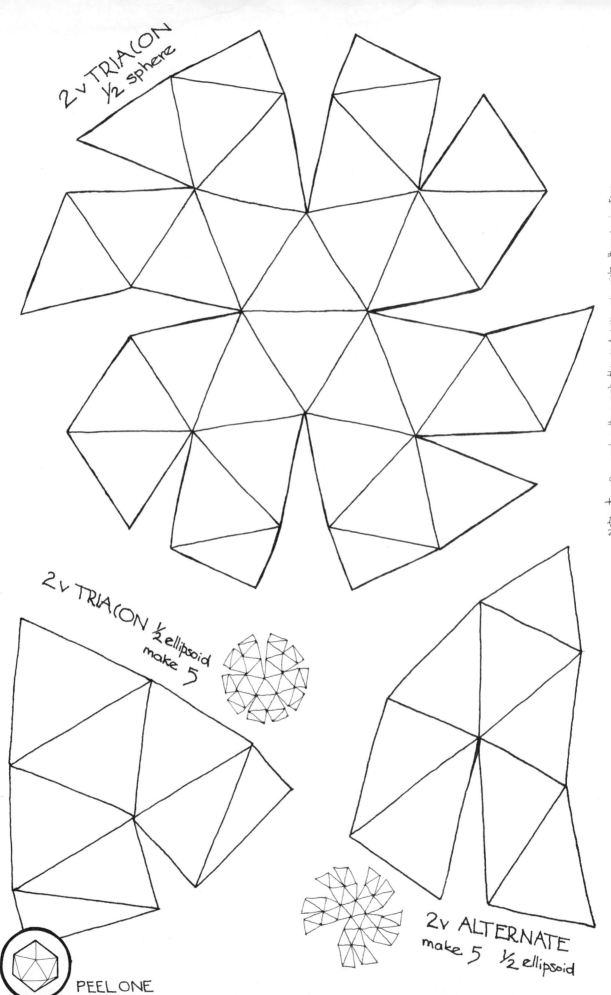

2v TRIACON
½ sphere

Note, transfer peel pattern onto thin card using pin pricks through junctions

2v TRIACON ½ ellipsoid
make 5

2v ALTERNATE
make 5   ½ ellipsoid

PEEL ONE

DOMES
STRUT AND JOINT.

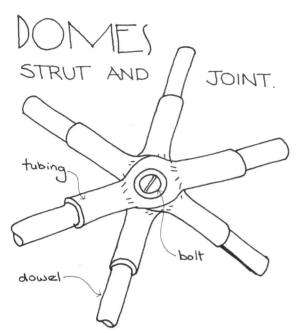

tubing

bolt

dowel

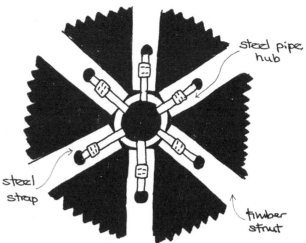

steel pipe hub

steel strap

timber strut

A special strapping tool must be hired

This is one of the simplest and most effective methods for light tent frames.

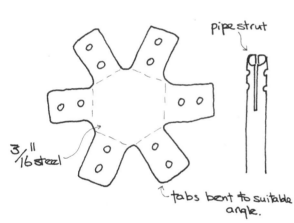

pipe strut

3/16" steel

tabs bent to suitable angle.

ply

8"

1"

Note: Hub may also be made from 6" diam 3/16" steel washer

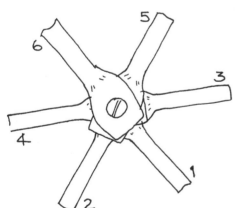

5
6
3
4
1
2

this diagram shows a method of jointing pipe struts directly to each other by flattening the ends and jointing through with a single bolt, numbers denote overlay sequence. Flatten ends by squeezing in a big vice.

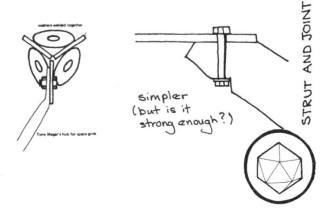

washers welded together

Tony Magar's hub for space grids

simpler (but is it strong enough?)

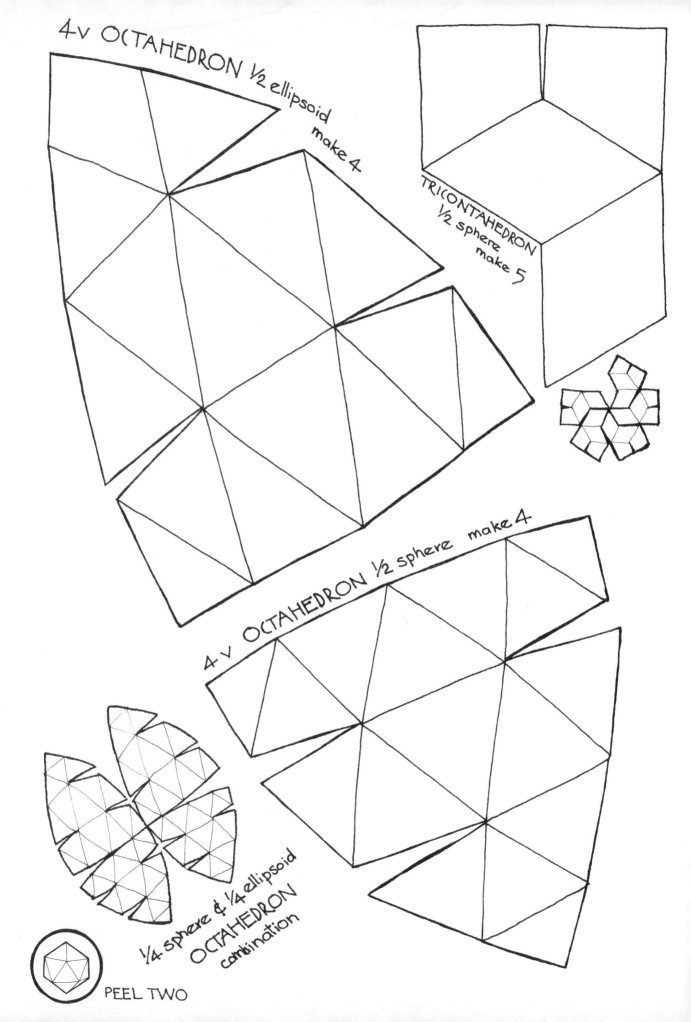

4v OCTAHEDRON ½ ellipsoid make 4

TRICONTAHEDRON ½ sphere make 5

4 v OCTAHEDRON ½ sphere make 4

¼ sphere & ¼ ellipsoid OCTAHEDRON combination

PEEL TWO

DOME

UNIT CONSTRUCTION

triangles are prefabricated separately.

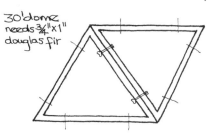

30' dome needs 3/4"x1" douglas fir

units fixed together with staples, glue or bolts and wing nuts.

for flush joints timber must be cut slant.
one way to get this slant is to rip a twice as big timber in half at an angle.

saw here

4"x2" timber

7° angle cut for a 3 frequency 30' dome.

rough guide strut width/length = 1/24

ply or metal plate strengthens corner

Note: use a jig for bolt hole drilling or drill on site.

cut tip angles on a jig e.g.

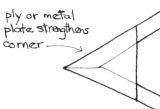

Radial saw

Angle: use an adjustable protractor to double check the saw's gauge. Hold it against fence, pull blade out and check to see that blade parallels protractor.

Length: tape measures are made to hook over a piece of wood. For greater accuracy, use the 1" line on the tape measure and line it up with inside of saw blade. Add 1" to total measurement when setting stop. V-mark stop and table and check the stop for slipping periodically while sawing.

Make sure table and fence are made of clear straight wood. Close one eye and sight down the fence.

CLADDING. will depend on available materials and other conditions but might include: plywood, PVC, polythene, cardboard, boarding.
The skin could be double with insulation sandwiched between. A reflective metallised surface will also give insulation.

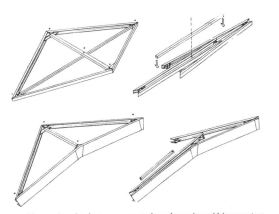

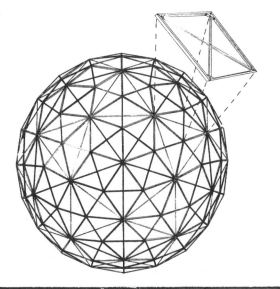

Diamond packaging sequence, an ingenious pin and hinge system allows diamond components to partially disassemble reducing packagin volume, typical diamond and base support shown.
A Fuller Research Foundation Project

other ways of making end joints

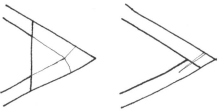

another method of getting a close joint between ribs

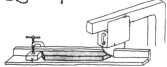

THIN SHEET DOMES.

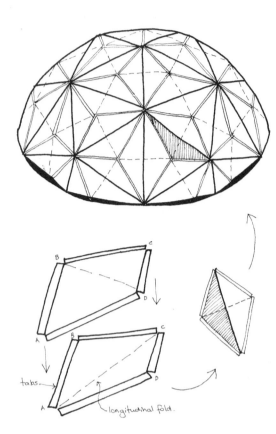

Thin sheet metal and cardboard are the cheapest thin sheet materials available. Steel is strong but cardboard although weak is better insulating and may be strengthened with fibreglass (cost goes up.)

The Domebook people made a 24' diam. dome with only 300 lb of Aluminium No3003 0.025" thick. The complete ½ sphere dome weighed only 600 lbs. Panels were cut out similarly to the car top dome on the right, but panel joining detail is more sophisticated.

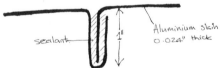

This means taking special care with templates as ½ of the edges are being overlapped by the other half. ie. some have bigger tabs than others. make a model!

NB? They had their seams on the inside of the dome. I would have thought that if they'd had them on the outside, it would have saved sealing and caulking except at vertices and bolt holes.

A clip punch or pop rivet gun is an alternative to bolting.

THIN SHEET.

Drop City Car Top Domes

"If you cut carefully around the edge you can get a 3½' x 7' sheet of 27 gauge steel with a baked on enamel surface from each car, 3½' x 9' from station wagons. Droppers loved station wagons and panel trucks sent us into paroxysms of ecstasy."
Peter Rabbit.

car top cut out with ax

flexible plywood pattern on car top

painted side up

panel cut and drilled

panel, cut, drilled and broken

When you are putting up a dome panel by panel you often have to use poles to support the wobbly sides as they close in toward the center. When we were putting up the second to last panel in the shop dome we had three poles in strategic spots to hold the wobbly overhanging panels from collapsing. The poles were nailed at the top so they wouldn't fall away if during a moment's strain the load were lifted up and off of them. The panel was an 8' by 19' and extremely heavy. We put it up with an inadequate crew, two men and two women. We struggled for an entire afternoon the last few inches Albert Maher pushed from on top of a spool resting on top of the cab of his pickup which we had driven into the dome. It was touch and go, a clamp might slip, Albert might collapse, the poles might buckle. Each one of many failures seemed equally as probable as getting the monster joined to the neighboring panels A huge shove, some quick work with the crow bar and clamps—Albert eased off and it still held, I took a few more turns on one clamp and added another one—it was a sure thing, we had it in place!

It felt as if the panel had been lifted into place by some incredible wave we had created that now washed back as we put down tools and Albert got down off the cab. But there was one last thing to check—the poles, were they dangerously bowed under this new load. The entire sensation in my head began for a moment to turn inside out when Holly yelled "look at them" but then I saw what it was— the dome was finding its shape, it had lifted all three heavy poles off the floor, they were hanging from where they had been toe nailed at their tops, swaying slowly. Three important pillars transformed in one moment into three dangling slow swinging pendulums.

Steve Baer Dome cookbook

DOME SEALING

As the whole skin, in a dome, is 'roof' sealing all the seams well is critical. Particularly with materials that shrink and expand and contract with wet and dry, hot and cold.

Methods of Sealing

— A membrane sprayed over the entire dome surface — rigid such as fibreglass (expensive but good) or flexible such as a butyl based weather topping. Applied with a roller.

— Shingling. either with wood or composite or metal; or by shingling the edges of the actual triangles to shed water.

— Caulks which fill the joints between triangles, adhering well.

— Tapes which span the joints gripping triangle edges (smooth)

— Gaskets which are sandwiched between panels

Caulks.

good adherence with flexibility is what you need so check chemical compatibility of the caulk with the dome materials.

The depth of the sealant should be less than ½ its width — joint design is important. A backup strip of P.V.C., sponged polyurethane, polyethylene foam or metal foil makes for narrower, concave and better seal.

Most caulking requires a primer esp. silicone based caulk.

Always start caulking from the bottom pushing the caulk in.

Tapes

1. Rigid. Fibreglass tape has been known to develop hair line cracks. but is usually good. The best method is to use a fibre glass resin filler as a caulk then the fibreglass mat strip over the joint.

2. Flexible. only the best P.V.C. pipe wrap tape will do of the common pressure sensitive tapes.

There are other sealant tapes on the general market for sealing greenhouses etc. often with Aluminium foil backing.

a well sealed outfit from Domebook II.

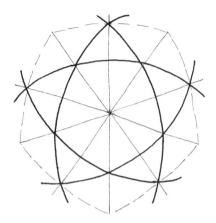

A Greater Circle is the largest circle
you can draw on a sphere.
A Greater Circle is a line drawn
around a sphere that defines two
hemispheres.
A Greater Circle is the shortest distance
around a sphere.
All the lines in the above diagrammatic
view of a sphere are Greater circles.
Such triangulated systems of Greater Circles
have good structural properties. By this
I mean that they use the least amount
of material to form a strong frame.

Making models using Greater Circles will
give you insight into geodesic geometry.
Full size frames may be made of 4"
wide strips of flexible plywood, 8' long,
bolted together at regular intervals or
another method is to use flexible bamboo.

Glastonbury 1971.

Greater circle configurations of
thin bamboo lashed together with
garden string make light, strong,
available, low cost (if rather slow
to erect) tent frames. This is
really a geodesic solution to the
frame of the traditional gypsy
'Bender' tent; which is covered in
layers of felt and scrap materials
to make a warm and comfortable
dwelling.

PLYWOOD PODS

Peel Dome ——— suitable for smaller domes. Plywood comes in 4' widths, so a regular polygon floor frame with 8–16 4' sides is made.

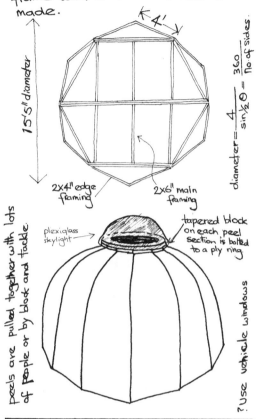

↑ 4'

$\sin \frac{1}{2}\theta = \frac{360}{\text{No. of sides}}$

15'5" diameter

diameter = $\frac{4}{\sin \frac{1}{2}\theta}$ = $\frac{360}{\text{No. of sides}}$

2x4" edge framing

2x6" main framing

plexiglass skylight

tapered block on each peel section is bolted to a ply ring

peels are pulled together with lots of people or by block and tackle.

*Use vehicle windows

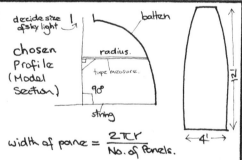

decide size of skylight

batten

chosen Profile (Model Section)

radius.

tape measure.

90°

string

12'

← 4' →

width of pane = $\frac{2\pi r}{\text{No. of Panels}}$

CUTTING PEELS RIGHT

Stake out the profile of the shape you want with a flexible batten 12' long. Measure radii at foot intervals along the batten from this life size model section. From these radii you can measure the circumference at that point and hence the width of the panel. These widths can then be used to make a full size pattern in card. It must be very accurate or you'll have gaps (which may be covered with a flexible beading—only small gaps.)

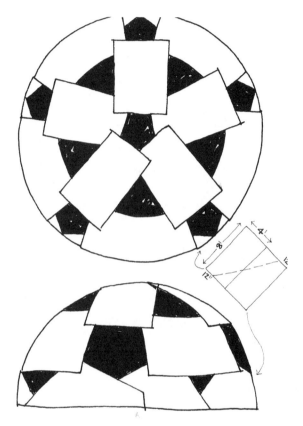

4'

8

12

Fuller Patent Shingle Dome Uses mainly full sheets of 8x4' ply. Minimal cutting & fixing — many 'windows'!

The 'Domebook Dome' ply skin.

PODS

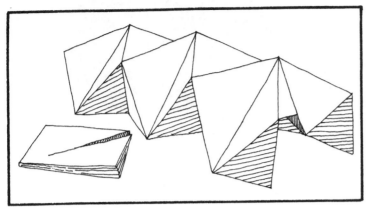

FOLDING THIN SHEET STRUCTURES

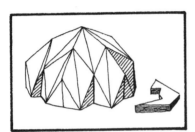

Folding from a single flat sheet of paper. Its amazing the no. of strong structures that you can devise.

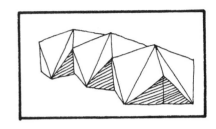

Because of the consistent geometry the domes shown on the left may be used to close the ends of the barrel vaults shown on the right.

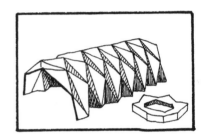

This is one of the simpler structures. Illustrated here in model form and full size.
Made of triple wall cardboard it is 8' square 6' high; folds down to a 5'6" square 4" deep, or with a zip on one of the vertices, into a triangle ½ the size and 8" deep. It weighs around 40 lbs will sleep 6 people, is easily stored, warm and disposable.

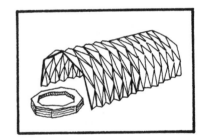

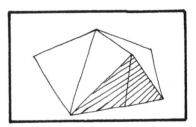

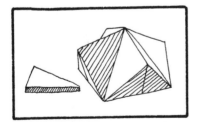

FOLDING GEOMETRY.

Many sheet materials might be used — including Triwall cardboard, sheet steel, sheet Aluminium, plywood, plastic foams, rigid plastic sheets, paper board etc.

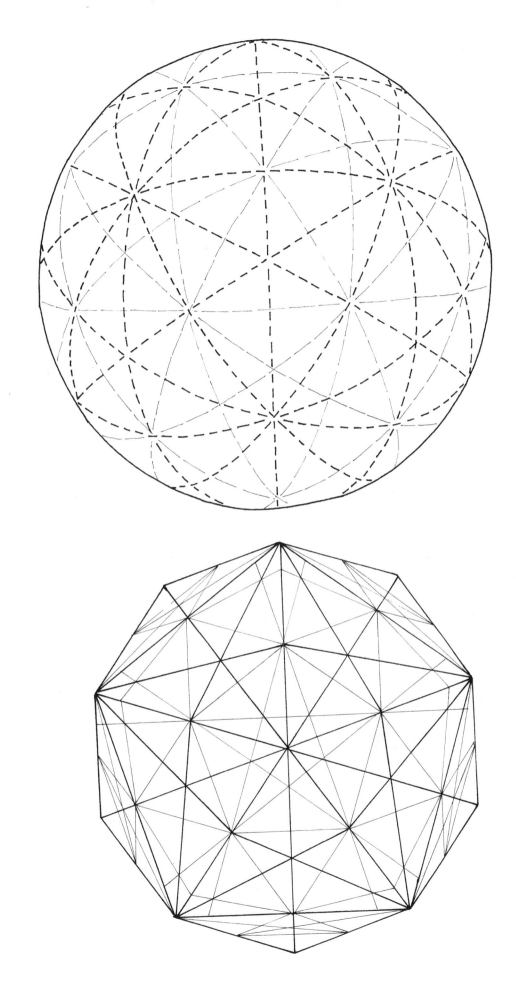

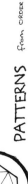

PATTERNS from ORDER IN SPACE by Keith Critchlow

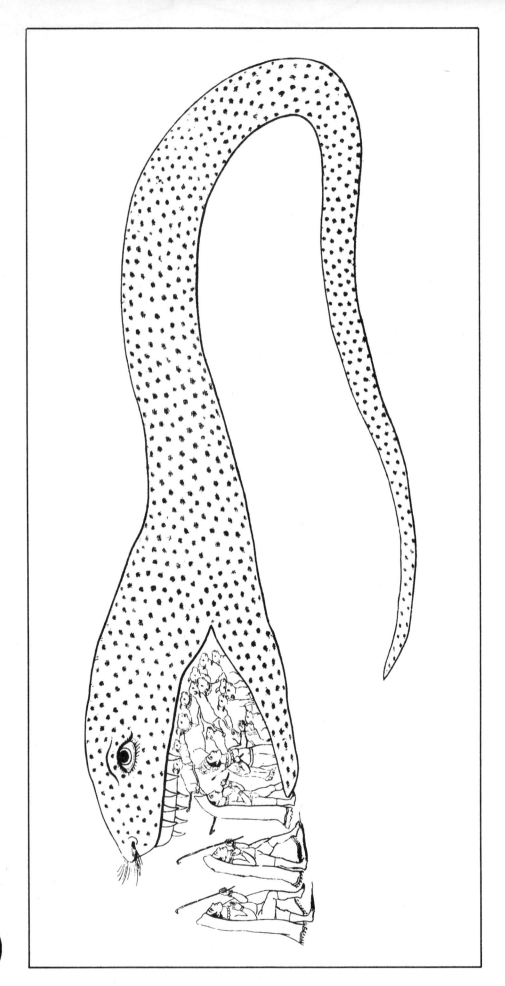

don't be boxed in

Build Your Own

energy
materials
imagination

Resort to ecological principles: MONEY DOES NOT EXIST. ONLY:

Energy, perseverence and imagination are needed but these resources are limitless—unaffected by the laws of supply and demand.

So go ahead and DO IT.

Pay homage to the SUN—the original source of all your energy.

No one can tell you the WAY to build a dome or a zome or whatever.

CREATE.

You are your own architect. Work with what you have—ENERGY—and scrounge the rest.

Play with models. Experiment. Use stiff cardboard cut into geometric shapes and taped.

Get your energy going and the dome's SYNERGY will carry you.

SCAVENGE AND SCROUNGE.

As Amerika rots in its garbage, you can survive on the waste.

Materials can be had from schools, construction projects, demolition sites, people, industry, lumber yards. Much is laying around dumped. Pig Amerika, in its greed, will give us our sustenance.

From dead cars in junk yards you can get valuable metal tops, sometimes just for the effort.

More information can be found in libraries and government documents. Check the Whole Earth Catalog.

Ideas are free and the energy is there.

Liberate YOUR ecosystem.

Ecology begins with yourSELF.

JOE HRYVNIAK

We are at a college. A commune—Libre—visited here and turned us on. Now we have a 22 foot DOME added to our environment.

We got FREE: Tools, space, use of a station wagon, railroad ties, 2 by 4's, nails, fiber board, siding, paint, plastic skylight, money, and advice from a professor who built his own house.

We had no plans on how to build a dome in one hundred and seven easy steps—there are none. We did not know what we were doing when we started, but we learned a lot.

It will all be useful again for our survival in the coming environmental crisis.

Return to your MOTHER EARTH and live in a dome. Get, for a dollar: DOME COOKBOOK.

From: Lama Foundation
       Box 422
       Corrales
       New Mexico 87048

—or—

THE MOTHER EARTH NEWS

PAPER BUILDINGS

A HOUSE BUILT OF NEWSPAPERS.

"Fibreboard or cardboard (the almost totally taboo word in the west for structures) has many important features to recommend itself for the job of providing the worlds housing: It can be handled on an intermediate technology level it is a constantly renewable energy source (all green stuff could potentially become mulch); it is an indigenous commodity in most countries in raw form; it can be fabricated in many ways) even to using amino acids in the green leaves as a bonding and water--proofing element. Possible ways of manufacturing the mulch are either as mould panels made direct for a composite building system, in sheet form for customer cut panels, in complex sheet or corr--ugation types or into 'blocks'! Finally and not least cardboard can be recycled; back into the ecological cycle — as it is basically an organic material — or back into the pulping process to be repatterned.
There is nothing to prevent cardboard being a vehicle for other material systems — as reinforcement for mud or light concrete — we have successfully sprayed a hexagon house with gunite — or as a vehicle for thin g.r.p (fibreglass) which we have used on the octagon house."

extracts from an article by Keith Critchlow in 'The Paper House Review' Architectural Design October 1970.

"My big dream is still to make a paper mache house. Paper houses have been built in the orient for thousands of years using wheat paste and persimmon juice for water proofing.
Laminated newspaper soaked with wall paper paste is plenty strong enough if it can be water proofed.
Another way would be to make a mixer, like a cement mixer, for paper mache. The newspaper would be shredded and mixed with waterproof glue then poured into panel forms along with willow branches or cattail reeds from the swamps (?) and then pressed with heavy weights into a light strong panel of paper mache. Then to cinch it and seal it a laminated paper face would be applied to front and back."

John Verndale
Domebook II p.60.

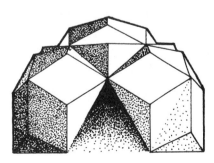

D.G.Emmerich.

120 identical units enclose 15m³ packed flat it takes up 2 m³.

PAPER HOUSE ONE

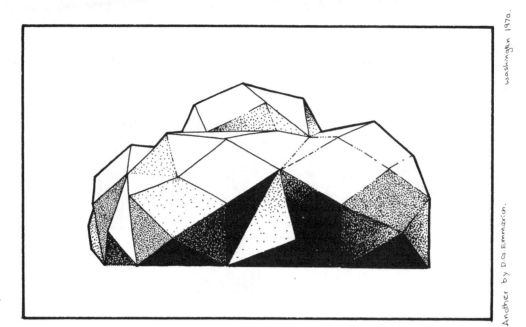

Simple Paper Pod Recipe.

"Obtain sufficient cardboard (of the type with two flat sheets outside and a corrugated piece in the middle) from large cardboard boxes from shops selling washing machines and other big products such as radiograms or T.V. sets or better still go to the cardboard factory direct & get the card--board before it is made up into boxes.

Cut out 30 equilateral triangles of cardboard, the larger the better— —4! sides are ideal and will produce a dome which gives you good head room — leave an inch flap on all three sides. At this stage you may paste silver foil on the inside of the triangles so they reflect heat and light from inside the dome — then if you stand in the dome in front of the foil, you can feel your own body heat reflected— —the dome acts like a concave reflector with all its facets angle back at you.

Bend the inch flap in on all 3 sides (for stapling together) Paint on a first coat of oil based, polyurethane or plastic emulsion paint. Staple the flaps together with a heavy industrial ½" stapler———

— Staple them together in groups of five triangles to make up 3 dime- -nsional pentagons. 6 of these pentagons go to make up your half sphere.

When you stand the ½ sphere on the ground you will notice its standing on 5 points. Cut off half the length of the points and staple the bits you've cut off in the gaps, and you've got a perfectly flat bottom.

Give another coat of paint, let it run down the cracks to make the dome waterproof. (You may have to add waterproof tape or a sealing compound if it leaks) If you use white paint it will look really spacy."

Martin
Project Free London.

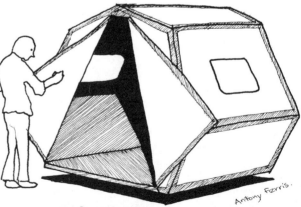

Antony Farris.

made of a sandwich board with rigid urethane core and kraft paper skin 7'x8'x7' high weighs 80lbs uses production size standard panels.

PAPER TWO

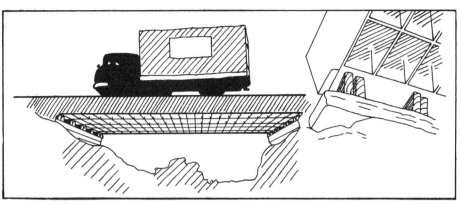

The truck weighs 5 tons. The bridge is cardboard.
A sandwich panel of card and fibreboard tubes forms
the surface, supported on a simple egg-crate type
structure. An advertising stunt for International Paper Inc.

Of course such feats as shown
above need careful calculation
Yet it is simple for a 'novice'
to build paper structures if he
starts with inherently strong geomet-
-rical forms — the polyhedral solids.
described in the book 'Order in Space'
by Keith Critchlow.

This Hexagon house by Keith Critchlow
is a 6M diameter polyhedron
utilising a standard triangulated set
of panels together with timber door
and window inserts. It is made in
Tri-wall pak a laminate of 3 layers of
board which is 13 mm thick and has
the equivalent thermal insulation to
that of a 14" brick wall. The board
is coated with a waterproof finish
but for more permanence it can be
sprayed with concrete. With the
standard varnish finish the shelter
should have a minimum life span
of 18 months. It could also be faced
with a flame resistant resin reinforced
coating extending the lifespan to 10 years.

The floor can be concrete or timber
or the structure can be pegged
straight to the ground. It can be
erected in one day and easily built
in clusters. Maximum height 13'6"
maximum width 19'8" weight 700lb
crated dimension 13'6" x 6'6" x 1'6"
A similar structure derived from the
octagon has a maximum diam. 25!

To Bend Cardboard first score,
with a tool like this,

3/8" eyebolt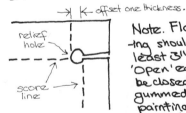

on the side you want to fold towards.
If you are folding it 180° onto
itself 2 lines need to be scored
a board thickness apart.

→ |← offset one thickness.

relief
hole

score
line

Note. Flaps for glue
-ing should be at
least 3" wide.
'Open' edges should
be closed with
gummed tape before
painting or assembly.

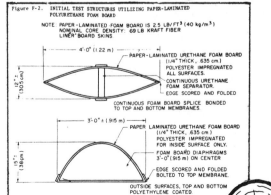

Figure F-2. INITIAL TEST STRUCTURES UTILIZING PAPER-LAMINATED
POLYURETHANE FOAM BOARD

NOTE PAPER-LAMINATED-FOAM BOARD IS 2.5 LB/FT³ (40 kg/m³)
NOMINAL CORE DENSITY: 69 LB KRAFT FIBER
LINER' BOARD SKINS.

4'-0" (1.22 m)

12"±
(30.5 cm)

PAPER-LAMINATED URETHANE FOAM BOARD
(1/4" THICK, .635 cm.)
POLYESTER IMPREGNATED
ALL SURFACES.

CONTINUOUS URETHANE
FOAM SEPARATOR.

EDGE SCORED AND FOLDED

CONTINUOUS FOAM BOARD SPLICE BONDED
TO TOP AND BOTTOM MEMBRANES.

3'-0" ± (.915 m)

15"±
(38cm)

PAPER LAMINATED URETHANE FOAM BOARD
(1/4" THICK, .635 cm.)
POLYESTER IMPREGNATED
FOR INSIDE SURFACE ONLY.

FOAM BOARD DIAPHRAGMS
3'-0" (.915 m) ON CENTER

EDGE SCORED AND FOLDED
BOLTED TO TOP MEMBRANE

OUTSIDE SURFACES, TOP AND BOTTOM
POLYETHYLENE COATED.

PAPER THREE

LOG CABINS

Cut down the logs you use; or pit props, telegraph poles, railway sleepers, other available surplus/waste log timber. If possible cut only standing dead trees or thin out overcrowded parts of your wood. Always plant more trees than you cut down.

Use trees that are straight and not tapered. Trees adjacent to the cabin will provide windbreak and shade, but remember the roots of a tree extend about the same distance from the trunk as do the branches.

If there are no stones, use concrete or soil-cement. Wood posts treated with concrete or some other wood preservative (old crankcase oil might work.)

The floor frame is then erected to form a firm base for the walls. Locate used doors and windows on this and make framing for them. Now the walls. Each log set down should be notched on the underside and set on top of the log going the other way. Nails are used to steady logs to door and window framing but should not be necessary on the corners.

The roof may be covered with used boarding, doors, split logs etc. and then covered in three layers of tar paper roofing, caulking all seams well. Make sure you give a good over-hang to the eaves, unless you are using gutters.

Filling in the gaps between logs, called chinking is done best with soil cement mortar, moss, adobe, bark wood scraps or fibreglass.

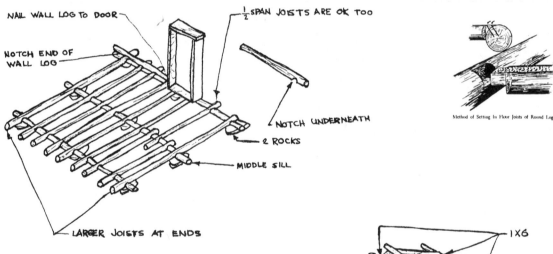

NAIL WALL LOG TO DOOR

½ SPAN JOISTS ARE OK TOO

NOTCH END OF WALL LOG

NOTCH UNDERNEATH

2 ROCKS

MIDDLE SILL

LARGER JOISTS AT ENDS

Method of Setting In Floor Joists of Round Logs

BASIC FRAMING

LOG CABIN ONE

Strip the bark to protect the logs from insects and rot and you are ready to build.

A good method of stone foundation for a small cabin is to dig holes down to a firm strata of the earth (often 2' will be enough) and fill with medium size stones, placing two large flat stones on top, bedded in soil.

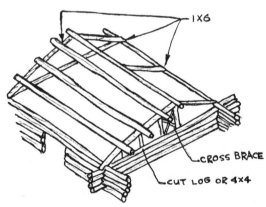

1X6

CROSS BRACE

CUT LOG OR 4X4

ROOF FRAMING

Roofing : In cold regions a high roof insulation is achieved by growing grass on the roof (shallow sloping) on a humus of pine needles. The layer of pine needles ensures that the pine roof does not rot or deteriorate. The roof framing must be substantial to support the added weight.

Another good roofing to use is of shakes. These are wood 'tiles' about 2'0" x 6" x 3/8" thick. They are split from larger timber blocks or short logs. For making shakes you can use second grade logs that are cracked or tapered (and therefore cheaper if you are buying).

A rented band-saw will make working with logs very much faster and easier and you can saw your own planks with a simple attachement.

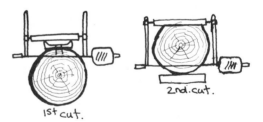

1st cut.   2nd cut.

Log cabins burn easily so be careful with your stove pipe or chimney details.

INSULATION SPACE   STOVE PIPE

LOG CABIN TWO

Fladdal, Thelemarken.

THATCHING

Thatch has much to recommend it as a roof covering, it is warm in the winter and cool in the summer and when the thatch has settled down the risk from fire is not great in country districts. It is not expensive as roofing but requires certain skill and ability to perform the thatching of a roof satisfactorily. Thatch is suitable for roofing all manner of garden erections and it is probably in this direction that the amateur may at first use it.

<u>Tools</u> a bill hook, an eaves knife or stout sheep shears, one or two hand rakes, ladders long enough to reach the roof ridge. also needed — a supply of pegs, binding cord, a wooden mallet, and some stout cord to carry the thatching material from ground to roof.

<u>Preparing the straw.</u> Norfolk reed is the best material but straw is extensively used in Somerset and Dorset. To begin with the material is made into bundles, this is then stacked on site. The straw is then soaked with water and compressed by treading. The straw should then be drawn from the bottom of the heap where the pressure is greatest. Loose portions are removed and the fingers are used to comb it perfectly straight. This 'yealm' of straw, which is as much as can be grasped in both hands, is tied at one end with straw from this same bundle.

<u>Two Methods of Thatching</u>
One is to lay a covering of fibrous turf over the roof and to push the straw through the turves while the other is to sew the straw directly onto the roof. With 'the turf method' 3" broad battens are nailed on the rafters at 6" centres. The turves, cut with tapering edges, are laid on the roof overlapping from the eaves up. The thatch is then fixed with the aid of staples in a similar manner. On the ridge turves are laid over the straw to form a well defined ridge or 'bolster.' Another method of finishing is with a tightly plaited straw roll.

With the second method of thatching similar battens are used and the straw sewn directly to the battens with sewing twine. The ridge is finished either with turves or with two wide boards the length of the ridge. This method is more common than the other as it is often impossible to obtain firm fibrous turf.

<u>Heather and Reeds.</u> Mainly confined to the north, Heather will make a very durable thatch; a similar method of laying to the second method described above (sewing with twine) is used. Many reeds are valuable roofing material the two methods described above being used. Broom may also be used in a similar manner to heather.

On the roof of a dwelling house 10 bundles or 5 cwt of straw will be required for each square of thatch (of 100 sq. ft.) If done expertly with finest quality wheat straw the roof should remain quite watertight for about 30 years or with reeds 40 years. If the work is done indiff-erently it may not last for more than ten years.

THATCHING.

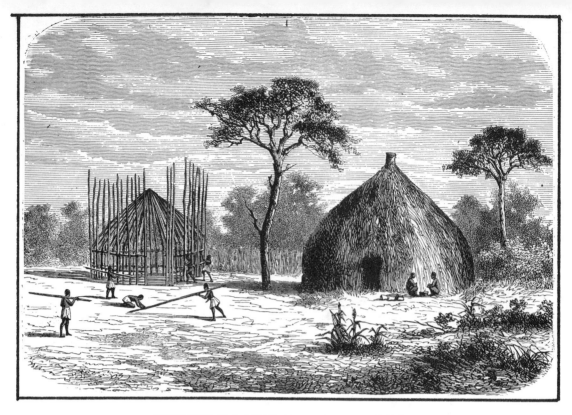

HUT-BUILDING IN A VILLAGE OF UHIYA, CENTRAL AFRICA.

VILLAGE IN LOVALÉ, WEST AFRICA.

TREE HOUSES

Consideration of the tree is primary. Decide on the tree that will best live with you. Test branches you are going to build onto by tieing a rope to them and getting half a dozen friends to hang onto the rope. When you are sure it is the tree you want to live with start thinking about the structure. Investigate birds nests, see how they relate to a trees structure. The construction is one of thin woven branches with a thin lining of adobe and a final lining of down. Notice that no nails are driven into the tree.

Although a structure like a very large birds nest could be built you would have to be sure that the tree could take the weight of so much mud. Better for a human sized tree house to use lighter weight materials.

For instance : a platform of timber prefabricated on the ground, winched into place, fastened either with bolt clamps or lashed with nylon ropes. see below.

The superstructure could be modelled on the wig wam and covered in bark or made of slabbing. (the outer cut off a log usually sold cheap as firewood at a timber yard.)

Indian Food Cache

Before you start building make a really good study of the tree. Climb it, swing from it, sketch it, photograph it, make measured drawings, sleep underneath it, and don't forget that lonesome trees attract light ning.

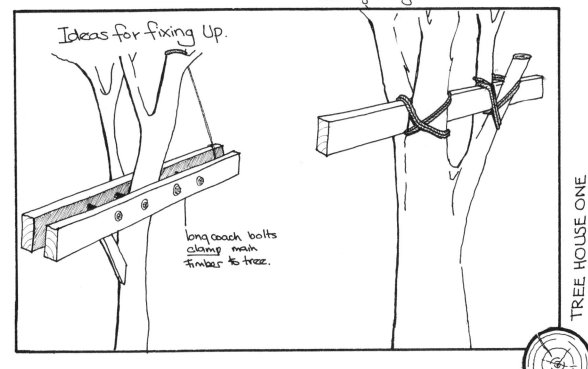

Ideas for fixing Up.

long coach bolts clamp main timber to tree.

TREE HOUSE ONE

210, Chapel Oak of Allouville, Normandy.—From a sketch by Marquis in 1824.

Whilst measuring the electrical
activity in plants with a lie detector
in 1966 a man called Clive Backster
noticed an electrical response in plants
to ideas within his own head.
For instance when he decided to cut
a branch off a plant the electrical
activity underwent startling increase.
To explore this phenomena he devised
a machine to drop live shrimps into
boiling water at random time intervals;
whilst in another room the electrical
activity of a plant was recorded.
It was discovered that the plant
'recorded' the exact moment of
each shrimps death.

TREE HOUSE TWO

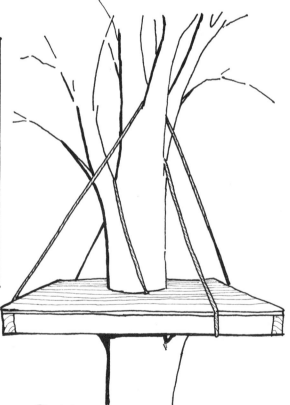

Platform Suspened on Nylon
Ropes or Steel Hawsers.

A DOBO OR TREE-HOUSE FOR UNMARRIED WOMEN IN MELANESIA.

In some places such tree-houses serve as refuges against marauding tribes. They are common on the New Guinea Coast.

BUSH HOUSE

Wind-swept hilly areas are often impossible to grow crops on but with the addition of lines of trees to shelter the land, arable farming is again possible.

Foliage can be used as shelter. The vegetation may be used on its own as with the arable land shelter belt mentioned above or in conjunction with other shelter forms. The Ivy covered country cottage will be warmer with its leafy companion. Plants grown against walls in town and country will increase insulation, provide fruit and soften the building aesthetically. It could also be a fire-escape from upper stories.

Topiary is the art of modelling trees and bushes and there seems no reason why you shouldn't <u>grow</u> your own house and trim it to shape. The bush would provide insulation, structure (to hold a water-proofing sheet of thin plastic to keep out the rain.) camouflage and possibly food. What are the regulations concerning bush dwellers?

Foliage is useful as a camouflage where a shelter is likely to be challanged. A bramble bush covering your dugout will ensure that nobody stumbles across the ventilation shaft.

photo by Kathy Collins.

'Use Blackberries, such as the Himalayan Giant, to cover banks, old sheds and other odd buildings.'
Pears Cyclopaedia.

BUSH HOUSE. TWO.

"It is perfectly possible to build geodesic domes with what I'll just call a trellis, a triangular trellis, that is too light for you to climb on and so forth, but plant your vines on it.......... then the vines themselves begin to bind up, and because these are the shortest lines the vines tend to follow them. They will fortify every line in the geodesic dome and the dome will simply grow and get stronger year after year, be bound to the earth and become a very extraordinary kind of forest bower. I found this appealing to a great many people around the world."
R.B.Fuller in Domebook II.

SHED

Basically a simple framing covered with some cladding: most often timber boarding. Easy to make from many available materials.

Legal Advantage

You can erect without Planning permissions or building regulations a building that is used for ——

1. During the day only and for non business purposes.
2. Not exceeding 1000 cu.ft.

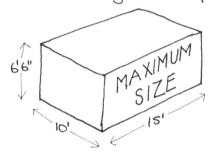

MAXIMUM SIZE

6'6" 10' 15'

3. Minimum of 6'0" from the house.
4. No heating Appliance with chimney or flue.
(These are only representative of local Bye Laws; look up those in your area specifically.)

Sheds might include tool sheds, potting sheds, bicycle sheds, green-houses, sun lounges, studios, workshops, playrooms etc.

This all means that you can greatly extend the capacity of a small house if there is a reasonably large garden or you can live in town in other peoples garden.

The 'SOLAR' summerhouse revolves to follow the sunlight or to turn away from the wind.

Sheds can be obtained very cheap secondhand; and often may be obtained free by dismantling and taking away. They are simple to modify or make from scrap or to move about. You can use planting around the shed to increase insulation and privacy: even live amongst your food in the greenhouse types. Greenhouse environmental control tecnology is well advanced and many sophistic--ated devices are on the market. (see Energy page   )

✳ No Planning Permission is necessary to build the floor/foundations if there are no permanent walls or roof. So you can lay a concrete 'floor' with service points and drainage ('yard', 'rock garden', 'sculpture!') and erect mobile or temporary superstructure when needed. Tree stumps will often make good foundations for sheds and cabins.

✳ Note. A planning permission request to build a 'nuclear bomb fallout shelter' could hardly be refused and could be a pleasant sound proof space with little waste of land ideal as a 'music room'.

✳ Another point is that temporary or mobile 'extensions' to the house of the type described above, do not effect the rateable value. So a small house may be enlarged without effecting rates.

SHED ONE.

SHED TWO

EARTH

INTRODUCTION

It is only in the last 100 years that earth has stopped being our major building material along with timber. Many thousands of 'mud huts' or houses of pisé de terre, still exist all over England and a decreasing amount of earth building has gone on up to the present day.

The photograph on the right shows my mother, grand mother and her mother outside the front door of our earth walled dwelling in Nottinghamshire in the 1930s. This cottage which was my great grand mothers was typical of an English working mans dwelling in the country.

Earth was always a good building material when properly used; but it should now be reconsidered as a primary building material since the tecnology of soil-cement has in recent years made its perform-ance reliably equivalent to that of brick or concrete for domestic architecture. Its advantages over the more commonly used materials are its cheapness and availability and the fact that it is a material well suited to self--build.

SOIL may be considered as a compound of solid matter, liquid matter (water.) and gaseous matter (air). Topsoil contains a large proportion of organic matter,— beneath this is the subsoil. It is the subsoil generally utilised as a building material. Its suitability will depend on its elementary properties.———— internal friction, cohesion, elast--icity, capillarity, texture, chemical composition (colour.)

These properties will depend on the relative proportions of its basic components ——— very coarse sand, coarse, medium and fine sand, silt and clay.

Little Lumon, Scarrington, Notts. 1929.

Why don't you hear anything these days about earth wall buildings?

Inasmuch as there is nothing in bare earth to sell, no commercial group can be found to extol its merits.

consider a hole in the ground—

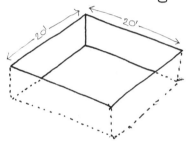

This might be the basement of a house, a pond for a fish farm, a cess pool, a rubbish pit ———— The subsoil material gained from this whole, if the earth is suitable, will make 18" thick exterior walls of a 2 storey house:——

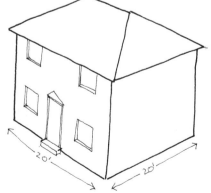

For structural purposes the walls could be much thinner but 18" gives excellent insulation. As great a range of styles of dwelling as with brick or concrete is possible.

Rubble & Turves	Turf huts of primitve design were still being built in England at the beginning of this century. See "The Charcoal Burners" hut Turf dwellings were usually rebuilt every few years.
Devon Cob	A monolithic mud technique that does without shuttering. Clay soil is well mixed and thrown into place. Sections of wall 18" high are built up; several days between each succesive section allow the wall to gain strength gradually. 2 ft. thick walls can support $1\frac{1}{2}$ tons per foot run or normal 2-storey construction. Questions of strength may be ignored by building walls of somewhat extravagant thickness. The surface must be protected by plastering (or some other coating) and sufficient damp-proof coursing at the foot of the wall and a generous overhang at the eaves must be given to achieve a durable wall.
Adobe blocks	Clay soil with a binder such as straw is made into bricks or blocks of various shapes & sizes. These are usually sun dried. The greatest strength will be achieved if a soil with at least 50% sand is used.
Wattle & Daub	A lime stabilised soil plaster onto wattle panels becomes a strong and comparatively light panel. These panels are usually set within a timber frame.
Rammed Earth or Pise de terre	Reports of rammed earth dwellings go back to Roman times when they were capable of earth structures that lasted for several centuries. The technique is to compact earth by ramming prepared soil in a shuttering. Compacted blocks may also be made.
Stabilised Earth or Soil-Cement	With an ideal soil and controlled conditions, this material is equal to brickwork & concrete for domestic architecture - and if locally available, is much cheaper. It is possible to construct cavity walls, floors, roof tiles and even lintels. The technique consists of carefully balancing the composition of the soil used and then adding a measured amount of lime or cement before compacting.

We admire primitive dwellings because we ourselves have lost the ability spontaneously to find the adequate expression for a building task.

Norberg-Schultz.

METHODS

FIELD TESTING YOUR EARTH.

General Tests

(a) Visual examination. This gives an idea of the proportion and size of the coarse granular components.

(b) Testing by Touch. A representative sample of soil with the very coarse particles removed (larger than 4.76 mm gravel.) The sample is rubbed between the fingers to establish the size of components.

(c) Sedimentation test. Take a clear glass bottle the mouth of which may be covered with a hand, cylindrical in shape and of at least ½ litre capacity. Soil is placed in the bottle up to ¼ of its depth; clear water is added up to ¾ of its depth and the bottle is left undisturbed until the soil is saturated with water. The bottle is then vigorously shaken and left to settle on a horizontal surface; after one hour the shaking is repeated. 45 minutes later the settlement of sand and silt will have taken place and the clay in water suspension will gradually settle at the rate of 12mm per hour. After 8 hours the different components, coarse sand, fine sand, silt and clay, are measured and compared.

A CHINESE FARMHOUSE

Tests of Fine Fraction.

(a) Shaking Test. to distinguish fine sand from silt or clay. The material for this test is obtained by syphoning off the water and material in suspension from the sedimentation bottle only 30 seconds after shaking up. This sample is then sedimented drained and evaporated in a separate container. The residue left is then rolled into a 2cm ball and struck several times between the palms of the hands. It will either have a smooth slippery appearance or there will be no change. The ball is then squeezed between the fingers of the other hand. The surface water may either dissappear or stay the same.
If water appears and dissappears rapidly it indicates fine sand or inorganic silt (a lack of plasticity)
If water appears and dissappears more slowly — a plastic silt or silty clay.

(b) Dry Strength Test. a ball similar to that used above is prepared and dried completely. Its resistance to crumbling between the fingers will vary in degree according to the fine components predominant in the soil. An easily pulverised ball denotes silt, fine sand and little clay. The more difficult it is to crush the more clay.

(c) Brightness Test. a quick test for the presence of clay. Cut a mass of rather moist soil with a knife. A bright surface indicates a plastic clay while an opaque surface indicates silt or sandy clay.

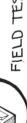

FIELD TESTS

SOIL STABILISATION

Despite its good insulating and weather resistant qualities, the use of simple compacted soil is vulnerable to moisture and the erosive effects of external agents. Resistance to these effects can be achieved by the addition of a stabilising agent.

Procedure: take soil (selected), pulverise it, add stabilising agent moisten carefully to achieve optimum moisture content for maximum unit weight, subject to heavy pressure (manually or mech-anically.) to restore original cohes-ion.

Methods of Stabilisation:

(a) Consolidation: Some natural soils require the addition of one or other of the basic soil components before they can be consolidated. i.e. to a clay-soil a calculated amount of sand may be added.

(b) Waterproofing: Addition of bituminous materials such as asphalt or pitch. This stabilisation method gives very effective results with cohesive soils made up of fine particles, which do not pulverise or mix easily, provided that a suitable mechanical mixer is used. drawback —— in some cases bituminous materials are vulnerable to the effects of soil bacteria.

(c) Chemical Treatement: Addition of substances such as lime, sodium silicate and calcium chloride. In order to change soils most successfully with chemicals it is necessary to know their chemical composition.

(d) Addition of a Binding Agent: Usually Portland Cement. (lime also produces this effect.) By this method a material of great strength may be made. This is known as :— Soil-Cement. The proper soil for stabilisation with cement is one which gives high strength and does not shrink appreciably when dried. An ideal soil must be very compactable and consist of a mixture of sand, silt and clay. The latter two in such a proportion to give the mixture sufficient cohesion and good granular composition without harmful shrink-age.

The optimum proportion is 75% sand and 25% silt and clay. Clay content should not be less than 10%. Soils with 45% sand 55% silt. clay to soils with 80% sand and 20% silt. clay are suitable for Soil-cement construction. About 80% of soils in Britain are suitable for some type of soil construction.

SOIL-CEMENT PREPARATION

Soils around the site are tested and the most suitable soil is select--ed.
The soil is spread in shallow layers on a smooth surface to dry. ie rain protection essential. No water should be able to be squeezed from a handful of prepared soil. The dried soil is then sieved and stored in a damp proof place.

Type of soil	% of cement
sandy	5——9
silty	8——12½
clay	12½——15

Note: Clay soils with more clay than 25% have a strong tendency to crack and shrink. Clay soils are also difficult to pulverise mix and moisten. A carefully measured amount of sand may be added.

Water: The amount of water is that needed to hydrate the cement, to give the mixture optimum moisture content and to facilitate the maximum compaction of the soil. Broadly the total amount of water should vary between 8 and 16% by volume depending on the soil.

Mixing the Components:
spreading the soil out in a layer of about 4" on a good impervious mixing base. The cement is sprinkled on and then thoroughly mixed by hand or by mechanical mixer.
The water is added in similar fashion with the aid of a watering can and sprinkler rose. Correct amount of water may be determined by squeezing a handful of the mixture in the hand. It should retain its shape without soiling the hand and can be pulled apart without disintegrating; on dropping from waist height onto a hard surface it should disintegrate into loose material.

N.B. Compaction, which may be done in a form or mould, must be carried out within 2 hours of moistening the mixture.

Compaction.
Shuttering Method: 6" of loose material is compacted with a metal or wooden rammer with a 3" square base until the strokes of the rammer produce a clear metallic sound.
When a section is completed and the shuttering removed it should be covered in damp sacking for 3 days to cure before adding the next section.
Note: a hand rammer will be between 12 — 20 lbs weight or may be pneumatically powered.

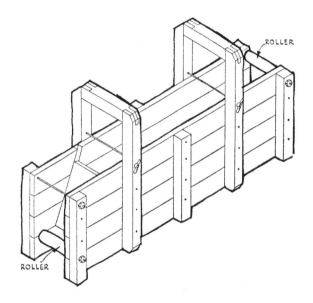

ROLLER

ROLLER

Simple Moulds: usually consist of four strong sides and a 'pusher' to slide the compacted block from the mould. Blocks should be kept moist the first 8 days after being made. After 21 days they achieve full strength and max. shrinkage. With large scale work is being planned it is necessary to make test blocks before starting.

Comparative Tests.
(a) the 'maximum unit weight' is directly proportional to strength and durability.
(b) On being struck with a hammer a metallic sound is produced.
(c) A 4" nail, hand held, should not be able to make cavities in the surface more than ¼" deep.
(d) Edges should be sharp and firm.
(e) No dimensional changes should occur.
(f) 8 hours under water should have no effect of breaking up the block.
(g) tensile strength

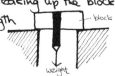

block

weight

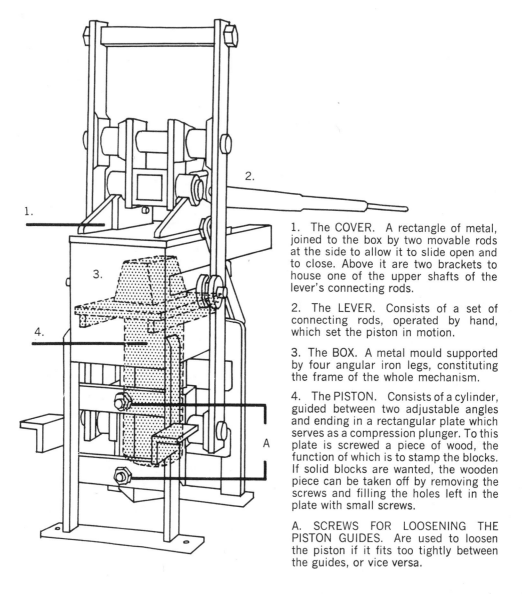

1. The COVER. A rectangle of metal, joined to the box by two movable rods at the side to allow it to slide open and to close. Above it are two brackets to house one of the upper shafts of the lever's connecting rods.

2. The LEVER. Consists of a set of connecting rods, operated by hand, which set the piston in motion.

3. The BOX. A metal mould supported by four angular iron legs, constituting the frame of the whole mechanism.

4. The PISTON. Consists of a cylinder, guided between two adjustable angles and ending in a rectangular plate which serves as a compression plunger. To this plate is screwed a piece of wood, the function of which is to stamp the blocks. If solid blocks are wanted, the wooden piece can be taken off by removing the screws and filling the holes left in the plate with small screws.

A. SCREWS FOR LOOSENING THE PISTON GUIDES. Are used to loosen the piston if it fits too tightly between the guides, or vice versa.

Fig. 36   CINVA-RAM moulder for the production of soil-cement blocks: explanatory sketch.

SOIL CEMENT
BUILDING DETAILS

Foundations : In a well drained site the foundations may be of earth rammed without shuttering laid on a shallow layer of small stones and stabilised by cement in the ratio 1 : 10 by volume. Other sites might use 'Cyclopean Concrete' which is large washed stones laid into the concrete.

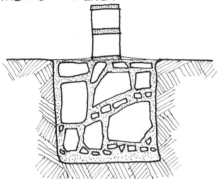

Cyclopean Concrete Foundation

Walling. : Damp Proof Course

1/ Waterproof cement mortar. (cement : sand — 1 : 2 + waterproof agent.) laid in a continuous layer ½" in depth.

2/ Bitumen. 2 coats of hot bitumen.

3/ Bituminous felt.

It is important not to use high strength soil-cement blocks with weak mortar or weak blocks with a strong mortar. The blocks should be wetted before applying mortar as absorption by the blocks can interfere with the setting of mortar. Mortar may be cement, cement and lime, soil-cement or soil-cement and lime.

Roofing in Soil-cement . . : Timber lathing or reeds are laid on the roof trusses and nailed down. A plastic mortar of cement and sandy soil, with vegetable fibres 3cm in length added as reinforcement in the proportion of 1 : 4 of mortar. The mortar layer should be laid 3cm deep. The smoothed surface, after being allowed to dry and harden is given 2 or 3 coats of bituminous material. A sprinkling of small gravel over the last layer of bitumen will improve durability.

Note. the roof may be 'reinforced' with barbed wire stretched across the roof laid between layers of mortar.

Flooring : The intended floor area is smoothed off and compacted by ramming the soil adequately moistened and with gravel added. A 5cm. 2" layer of soil cement mortar is then laid. When dry the floor is finished by sprinkling with water and dusting with dry cement —which may be colored.

Generally soil-cement building details may be similar to those traditionally used in brick building. With unstab- -ilised soil however more care has to be taken esp. in cases of localised loadings such as where joists are supported in the wall. It is necessary to reinforce with timber, soil-cement or concrete at such points.

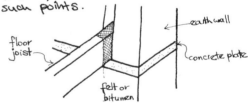

floor joist — earth wall — concrete plate — felt or bitumen

How To Make a Hand Rammer

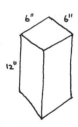

6" 6"

12"

ll

Hardwood block.

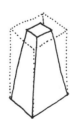

Taper to 3"x3" at one end.

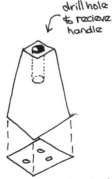

drill hole to recieve handle

6"x6"x¼" mild steel sole plate with counter sunk holes for screwing plate to block.

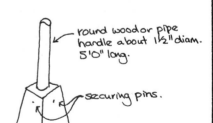

round wood or pipe handle about 1½" diam. 5'0" long.

securing pins.

If greater weight is required remove sole plate. Cut a cavity in base of block and fill with lead. Replace plate.

CHARCOAL BURNER'S TURF HUT.

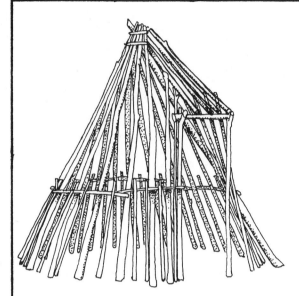

Mrs Langridge who built the hut illustrated here with her husband said that in her grandfathers family there would be four such huts serving as bedrooms — usually with two beds each — and a further long shaped hut would be the living room.

Cooking takes place over open fires outside — covered pans hung from a bar supported on tripods and an oven made of sheet metal covered in turf was heated, as were mediev--al baking ovens, by lighting faggots inside until heat built up, after which food would be sealed in to cook. Clothes drying Mrs. Langridge said was the biggest problem.

Huts of this kind might remain in use for up to about four years, but if the family left them for a time to work in another district, although they might return to the locality, the huts were made again and the old ones abandoned.

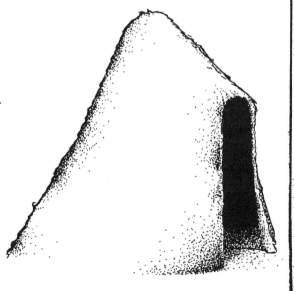

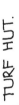

TURF HUT.

Exhibited at The Weald and Downland Open Air Museum, West Dean, Sussex.

WATTLE AND DAUB.

A 14C house exhibited at the Weald and Downland Open Air Museum, West Dean. Sussex.

The Medieval English House consisted of two bays; the one, in which the hearth was set open to the roof; the other with an upper chamber or solar above.

The people living in such a house had values, and a whole way of life that was so different from our own that it takes an effort of the imagination to appreciate it adequately.

The open hearth has many attractions if we think of a life lived mostly in the open air. The height of the hall prevented the kind of smoke congestion one might expect; all family life could be centred on the hearth more freely than in the next phase of development —— the big inglenooks.

The Welsh Farmhouse of the same era and construction contained both human and animal dwellings under one roof. There seems to have been no chimney or even special outlet for the open hearth peat fire.

Furniture was very simple and minimal: perhaps a table, bench, a few 3 leg stools, an oak chest and possibly a truckle bed.

A 15C Farmhouse from Denbighshire exhibited at the Welsh Folk Museum, St. Fagans, nr. Cardiff.

WORKABILITY OF SOILS USED AS CONSTRUCTION MATERIALS a/

NAME OF SOIL	PROPERTIES OF SOIL	
	Permeability when compacted	Suitability b/ as a construction material
Sand	Pervious	Excellent to fair
Silty sands	Semipervious to impervious	Fair
Clayey sands	Impervious	Good
Organic silt & very fine sands. Silty or clayey fine sands with slight plasticity.	Semipervious to impervious	Fair
Inorganic clays of low to mediumm plasticity. Sandy clays. Silty clays.	Impervious	Good to fair.
Organic silts. Organic clays of low plasticity.	Semipervious to impervious	Fair
Inorganic silts. Elastic silts.	Semipervious to impervious	Poor
Inorganic clays of high plasticity.	Impervious	Poor
Organic clays of medium to high plasticity.	Impervious	Poor

from Soil-Cement Its Use In Building. U.N. 1964.

a/ Extracted from the table given by the Bureau of Reclamation, in Unified Soil Classification System.

b/ Workability of a soil is the ease with which a given material can be handled or worked in a normal mixture, dry or moist, and ease of compaction.

Note on Identification: Soil is ribboned between thumb and finger where most sand soils cannot be ribboned, silt soils may be ribboned but have a broken appearance, whilst pure clay will form long thin flexible ribbons.

SOIL SUITABILITY TABLE

DUG OUT

Eskimo Dwelling

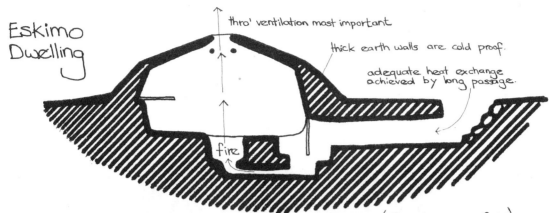

thro' ventilation most important

thick earth walls are cold proof.

adequate heat exchange achieved by long passage.

fire

These dwellings are kept warm in arctic conditions (often as warm as 80°F) using only small animal oil heating lamps. Through ventilation is carefully controlled.

The Frontier Dugout

The first and most desirable homes were simply small rooms dug into the south side of a low rolling hill. Walls were built up of sod blocks, holes being left for windows and doors which were usually bought from the nearest town or railroad point. Cotton wood poles laid side by side, then spread with a thick layer of prairie grass to provide insulation and prevent dirt sifting through formed the roof. Over this was carefully fitted a double layer of the sod building blocks. The grass soon got growing almost concealing the roof.

The floor of the dugout home was of rough wooden planks if the family could afford to buy them, otherwise it was treated as the neighbouring Indian squaws treated their tipi floors : sprinkled with water daily and swept with crude grass brooms until the surface was as hard and smooth as finished concrete.

Walls of the sod house were lined with newspapers pasted or pinned up with small, sharpened sticks to keep the dirt from brushing off. Some of the more ambitious families located outcrops of limestone rock which they burned and mixed with screened sand to make a plaster coating for the walls.

The dugouts were amazingly comfortable homes : cool in the summer, snug and easily heated in the winter. The thick sod walls and roof made excellent insulation in a day when few knew or appreciated the value of insulation. When properly located on the south side of a low hill, with adequate drainage to provide run off for rain and melting snow, the dugout was probably as comfortable a home as any of our pioneering fore fathers ever knew.

Canadian Whole Earth Almanac.
Shelter Issue   Winter 1970..

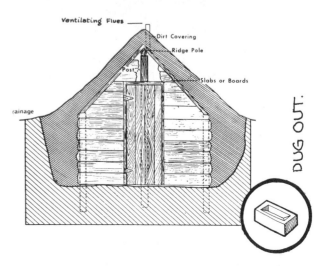

Ventilating Flues

Dirt Covering

Ridge Pole

Post

Slabs or Boards

Drainage

DUG OUT.

STONE

Drawn and Engraved by]   *The Cabin on the Moor—Evening.*   [Butterworth and Heath.

Methods of Walling

This is either carried out in courses like brickwork or a more or less indefinite manner known as random rubble. Rubble walls are built of thinly bedded stones of irregular shape, generally 9" deep or less. Block stone masonry is of squared blocks in regular courses or random formed of different shaped blocks.

The easiest walls for a novice to build are those of random rubble set dry. The foundations may be of concrete or a course of stout stones set with the greatest width across the wall and bedded to the solid earth. The stones are roughly selected for height and width, and arranged to fit into each other as tightly as possible. They are kept in line by setting them by a cord stretched from end to end of the wall.

Another type consists of several courses of stone then a few of brick; stones and brick being set in mortar. This adds strength to the wall.

Another method, particularly applicable to buildings, is to set rubble stones in front of a backing wall of brickwork. This has the effect of providing a smooth and durable inner surface. Each course is set in mortar and the stones are arranged to break joint. The face stones only are set in mortar; the space between these and the brickwork being filled with heating or small stones grouted in with liquid mortar. The mortar should not be allowed to run on the face of the stones.

All the foregoing walls can be put up by the amateur if reasonable care be taken to bed the stones well and work a bonder or through stone about every yard square of the wall surface. The bonder is a stone of sufficient proportions to pass through the wall from face to face and act as a stiffener to tie the whole together.

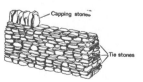

In cities built of stone, the mason had the central place in the building trades which in America is occupied by the carpenter. This plate is arranged to illustrate his different tasks in the construction of some grand house: (A) hoisting stones all cut to fit; (B) mortaring joints; (C) truing a footing; and (D and E) marking stones with rule and calipers and cutting them to measure. Almost lost in the background (G) is a mason sawing a large block. Various laborers mix mortar (F) and haul sand and plaster about (I,K).

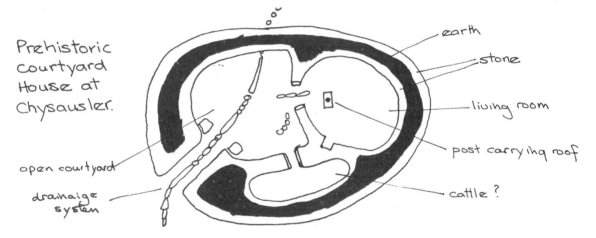

Prehistoric courtyard House at Chysausler.

earth
stone
living room
post carrying roof
cattle ?
open courtyard
drainaige system

STONE

Stones generally used are sandstones, limestone, slate and granite. The best stones are those that are free from bands or spots of colour and are of uniform structure. The stone is preferably cut to size and shape as soon as possible after quarrying, as it is more easily worked, but then set aside to season, gaining considerably in hardness and durability.

The amateur constructer will have to ascertain the type of stone available in his district, the cost of transport and the amount of work that will have to be expended on the stones before they are fit to use. As turned out by the country quarry the stone is split into thin slabs or sawn to suitable shape.

Cutting Stone

By no means easy until the knack has been aquired. One way is to score a shallow groove along all four faces with cold chisel and hammer then striking a few blows with the mallet through a board set vertically over the groove.

The working and tooling of stone, the arts of the mason are hardly to be acquired by the amateur but a few simple exercises will aid the shaping of capstones and the like.

Unmortared stone used for building purposes will have to be reasonably thick, well fitted together and secured where necessary by means of dowels, cramps or other fasteners.

Working with stone is satisfying and the results are beautiful, but it is slow work and needs some practice before a dwelling is attempted. Particularly worthwhile if stone is abundant and earth is scarce.

ORATORY AT GALLARUS, CO. KERRY.
Stokes, "Early Christian Art in Ireland."

MONASTIC CELL, SKELLIG MICHAEL.
Anderson, "Scotland in Early Christian Times."

FERROCEMENT.

Ferrocement is a high strength steel reinforced stucco that is easy to home make in any desired form. Developed by the Italian engineer Luigi Nervi, it has mainly seen use in the making of boat hulls; but it is well suited to all sorts of other monolithic thin shell enclosures. It differs from standard reinforced concrete in the amount of steel reinforcement, its subdivision, the density of the concrete and the method of construction. It is simple to use, needs few tools and little skill.

Method:
Using common sense structurally, any shape desired is framed with steel rod and then covered on both sides with several layers of steel mesh. A strong cement mix is then laid into this fine close mesh lattice.

Mesh:
The lattice mesh used is something similar to expanded metal or chicken wire. 1/8 — 1/4" rod is used to make the frame; or you can use a wooden frame, stapling the lattice to the timbers. Another method is to use a removeable timber frame that supports the rod, lattice and cement until it has cured.

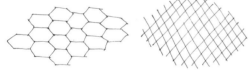

If you use chicken wire, which is one of the cheapest available meshes, use between 6 — 8 layers. Lay 4 layers inside the steel rod framework and 4 outside overlap all edges and stagger the layers tying it all well together. —— If you can push your little finger through it at any place its too open!

Sand: It should have a good even broad range of particle size, with no clay. Use 2 parts of dry sand to 1 part cement by weight.

Sharp sand! its important.

The whole unit, ie. hull of a boat or dome, should if possible be concreted in one continuous operation This might mean a day and night for a 20' semisphere dome with about 25 people working, so you need a large keen work force that you can trust.

When mixing the components be careful of adding exactly the right amount of water it is critical to the workability and strength. It must be stiff enough to hold onto the mesh but plastic enough to flow into all voids in the lattice. The amount of water will be around 3½ — 4 gallons per bag of cement. After being well mixed for about 5 minutes it should be plastic but hold together.

Work steadily from the top of the structure backing up with the large trowels from the inside.

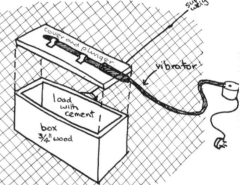

You can apply it with gloves but the mortar can't be as stiff and therefore will be less dense and will shrink more. Leave 1/8" cover to the mesh. When finished it must be covered with damp burlap or sprayed with a cement sealer to cure for 28 days.

CONCRETE

Concrete is composed of an aggregate and a matrix. Aggregate might be broken brick, river ballast (gravel) burnt ballast, broken granite, chalk, hard limestone, furnace clinkers and generally any hard unimflamm-able and non soluble materials. Aggregate should be of varying dimensions 1/8" — 1 1/2" clean and free from earth or organic matters. The matrix is lime or cement. Cement is a manufactured product containing 60% lime 20% silica 10% Alumina and small quantities of alkalis oxides and the like. It must be kept absolutely dry before use.

Proportions of Materials

foundations of small buildings : 1 part cement, 2 parts sand, 4 parts ballast.
Coke breeze blocks for walls : 1 part cement, 2 parts sand, 3 parts clinker.
Very strong cement for fine work : 1 part cement, 2 parts sand, 1 part fine ballast.
General Work : 1 part cement, 2 parts sand, 4 parts medium 3/4" ballast.

Shuttering. usually of timber.

Always thoroughly but uniformly ram and consolidate the concrete; leave the shuttering in place until the whole of the work has set. The surfaces may subsequently be finished by rough casting, plastering, mosaic tiling, pointing or in any desired manner.

Circular Work. Shuttering for circular work can be dealt with on similar lines, except that the shape will have to be derived by means of many narrow strips attached to a suitable skeleton or frame-work.

Moulding Blocks.

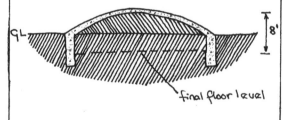

Tilt-up concrete construction is accomplished by casting wall panels on a concrete floor or other relatively smooth bed and then tilting them to a vertical position. To prevent bond with the wall panel the floor slab is covered with a plastic sheet or a chemical is sprayed on. wall panels are usually tilted by tractor or other lifting equipement. The panels are braced and reinforced concrete columns and are cast at the panel junctures to tie them together.

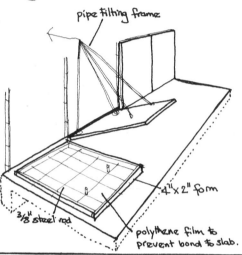

pipe tilting frame

3/8" steel rod

4" x 2" form

polythene film to prevent bond to slab.

Earthmould. Dwellings may be formed over heaped earth and into simple earth trenches. The earth is heaped and shaped as required then well tamped down. The concrete with necessary reinforcement is laid and then when the concrete has set the earth forming the mould is dug-out

GL

8'

final floor level

✳ consult an engineer for details.

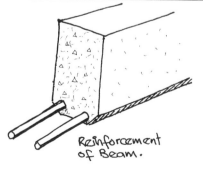

Reinforcement of Beam.

SOURCES OF MATERIALS
and the aesthetic of collaborated available resources.
(Using what's at hand.)

"They were forced to devise new ways of obtaining building materials, food and all the necessities of life...... The wall of a nearby farmhouse was made of tarpaper covered with chicken wire and sticks, bottle caps were used to hold the wire to the tarpaper. We did the same. Then we tarred over the stucco to waterproof it, and finished with a fibred aluminium coat. The windows were automobile glass. We learned how to scrounge materials, tear down abandoned buildings, use the unusable. Culled timber, railroad ties, damaged insulation, factory reject plywood, car tops. The garbage of America. Trapped inside a waste economy, man finds identity as a consumer. Outside the trap, he finds resources at his disposal...free. Things have value only in their use. Energy is transformed not lost."
Bill Voyd of Drop City.
from "Shelter and Society"
by Paul Oliver.

The City Dump. its got everything you need; but you are not usually
 allowed' to scavenge from a city dump. One must come to an agreement with the man in charge, who will usually solicit some small fee for overlooking your presence. Sundays and evenings are free often.

Skips. Those huge roadside bins. A trash trove.

Demolition Sites. When buying materials from a demolition site look for one away from the road. The more isolated the site, the cheaper the materials. Better still gain some experience and demolish yourself.

Motor Cars. Nowadays often a complete environmental package. A whole house could be made of parts from your local scrapyard.

Yellow Pages. Look up waste, salvage, demolition. Strategic value find out where and what your local industry is at.

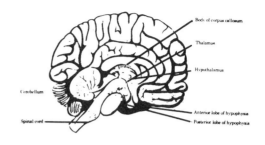

Industrial Waste. Almost every industry throws out something that is either fun or useful. Diplomatic approach necessary.

Finding. People often cannot be bothered to sell, leave lying about, you make low offer, and they are pleased to get rid of it. Keep a look out over peoples walls.

Auctions. Odd or unwanted things go cheap.

Army Surplus. Occasionally cheap.

Exchange and Mart. Useful for finding out current prices.

"Building materials are everywhere! not counting the natural elements - earth, rock, trees.... one can find salvage, culls, dunnage, scrap, junk and surplus items wherever you might look. One needs to learn the fine art of scrounging: keep an eternal eye out for materials. Haunt the junkyards and auctions, aquaint yourself with local building material industries. Offcuts, seconds etc., are common occurances in any high speed factory production. You can secure these misfit materials sometimes free for the hauling off.

The serious scavenger makes his first investment an oxy-acetylene torch and arcwelder. Scrap metal is relatively cheap and universally available; used corrugated iron may be reworked to meet a multitude of building needs: 5 gallon oil drums and iron pipe are low in cost, easily worked and versatile."
Ken Kern in "Owner Built
Home."

RECYCLE

Watch the patterns around you and work with them.

INSULATION

PRINCIPLES OF INSULATION

Air Separation (cellular ▓▓.)	Heat insulation good. Sound Insulation not so good. Almost any fibrous material may be used although a cellular material that does not allow the separate pockets of air to move is best.
Air Gap. //	Any air gap between two materials will greatly increase insulation. This may be achieved by building 2 leaf walls or by making the gap with another non structural material, such as thin polythene. The gap is best between ½" — 2" or convection currents in the gap will lower insulation value. Reasonable sound insulation. Condensation in the gap may be avoided by ventilation.
Vacuum ⋅nothing⋅	Any space that is evacuated will give almost perfect sound and heat insulation. There are always some losses from the edges or frame. Needs a very well sealed impervious cavity which tends to be costly.
Mass (low conductivity)	A thick wall of low conductive material will provide after a vacuum the best insulation of heat and sound. eg. 3 foot thick earth wall. (also good bomb blast insulation)

MATERIAL	ADVANTAGES.	DISADVANTAGES.
Glass fibre Quilt Mineral Wool Quilt Eel Grass Quilt	All these are approx. similar in performance/cost/availability. Glassfibre usually being the cheapest. The Quilts are non structural and need to be fixed in place. They come in bulky rolls and are simple to use. They are the lowest cost marketed insulation. Heat insulation good. Sound insulation not so good.	
Vermiculite fill (loose)	Similar performance/cost as polystyrene beads. May be poured into inaccessible cavities	Usually twice the cost of above Quilts. As it is loose it is only usable on flat surfaces or cavities.
Polystyrene Beads.	free `source`: shred polystyrene packing blocks.	" " Sound insulation with both these is not very high.
Polystyrene sheet	self-supporting, clean, easy to fix. Sound insulates fair. Heat insulation (4" thick) almost perfect.	note: be sure to buy non-flamable polystyrene.
Polyurethane foam sheet.		no equipement necessary but often more expensive than if foamed in situ (esp. large amounts)
Aluminium Foil	Reflects radiant heat well. cheap. Good as a back up to quilt or cardboard.	no sound insulation cold metallic feeling if exposed?
Corrugated cardboard. (also egg boxes, newspapers, etc.)	Can be collected for free. Even new its not expensive. 3 layers give the insulation of a cavity brick wall. Reasonable sound insulation. generally all paper is good insulation	Susceptable to damp & fire. Coatings get over these difficulties but raise cost.
Rugs. (hung on inside walls)	choice and cosy. dampen acoustics?	inflammable? expensive?
Windbreak. (such as hedge or ivy)	effective can be free or cheap. also food value? camouflage, cuts down noise, birds nest etc. + mysterious herbal properties?	slow to grow need attention
Dry Sand.	Very good sound and bombblast insulation. must be kept absolutely dry to give heat insulation	Heavy? tends to absorb moisture.

P.S. Postscript: should be another 'principle'. Reflection

Cultural enforcement is one of the factors that increases in a city along with density of people, complexity of services etc.

It is the enforcement situation which is likely to limit possible alternatives of shelter. Shelter in cities is a highly charged political issue and in the long-term it is only by political action that city dwellings will become responsive to their inhabitants, freely available to those who need them, beautiful etc. However, to the city survivor, there are alternatives that work in cities.

Methods mentioned in the checklist, not included in the text are attic conversion, roof-top development, room division. All methods rely on using existing space more efficiently.

Attic Conversion Many large city attics are unused. Need clearing out, flooring with ex.demolition floor boards (very cheap) and lining with similar cheap material. Make sure you have ventilation. The landlord will never know. A similar mobi le service equipment (calor gas or paraffin) is needed as with chronic squatting.

Roof-Top Development Tenement housing often has flat roofing. Domes, inflatables, paper pods almost any dwelling type in which the materials are easily transported upstairs may be used. Particular possibilities for inflatables and greenhouses.

Room division Old houses often have large rooms of 12 - 15 ft, high. Very cold in winter. Divide such rooms into compartments with scaffolding, old timber etc. Double or Treble density possible in such rooms.

Checklist Urban Alternatives

Short lease housing + commune housing. See overleaf.

Squatting. See this section legal.
Roof Top Development. See this page.

Attic development/conversion. See this page.

Garden Shed, Greenhouse. See the wood section.

Rain shell in the parks. Sleeping rough. See the tent section.

H Bomb Shelter. See shed.

Van. See mobile section.

Workmens Hut. See mobile section on trailer caravans.
Room Division. See this page.

Performing "Artists" Caravan. See mobile section on trailer caravans.
Crash-pads/dosshouses. phone BIT

Building given by councils etc., to bona fide organisation involved in "the Arts", social work, charity etc., for daytime office/workshop use, are often used as housing quarters (unofficially) by the workers.

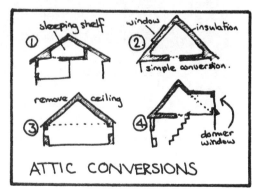

ATTIC CONVERSIONS

URBAN SHELTER

Student Community Housing in Campden Town, London negotiates with councils for the use of short-life housing that has been compulsorily purchased by councils. A short lease is arranged for two to ten years before the houses are up for re-development. In this way thousands of assorted people have been re-housed.

Temporarily available or simply derelict land would be used. Re-conditioned mobile units such as house boats and mobile houses which are readily available on the market, would be moved in.

Urban Communes have used similar techniques. Eel Pie Island, which was one of the most open and hectic communes ever seen in Britain, negotiated the rental of the derelict Eel Pie Hotel from its private owner.

If large numbers of people take action, housing prices can fall to nothing, which is how it should be.

EEL PIE ISLAND, TWICKENHAM

SHORT LEASE HOME

BUYING PROPERTY

There are many places that may
be bought for little if you
don't mind doing some work on
them, and being without the
usual amenities. Not all old
property is worth buying, it
depends on its situation and
structural condition. The ter-
raced house in a depressed industrial area, with few facilities
beyond water and a limited life
due to future development, are
the cheapest.

Finding. Decide on approximate
geographical location by study-
ing a good atlas and travelling.
Pick the strategic place. Buy
the local newspapers and study
the local scene. Estate agents
names may be obtained from these
newspapers. A local architect or
surveyor may be hired to look on
your behalf. You can advertise.
Lastly, and best of all for
cheap property, is the personal
search. There are many reasons
for homes being empty, so this
method can be quite exhausting
and time consuming. A little
persistence may find a way
round the reason for property
being empty; even a demolition
order might be quashed on ap-
peal. It is worth asking the advice
of a solicitor on such occasions.

Offer. On finding a property
you want an offer subject to
contract, survey, planning
permission or building li-
cense is made. A percentage
of the price being paid as a
refundable deposit. Payment
is best made through soli-
citors. Before completing
purchase, practical financial and legal investiga-
tions must be made.

Practical Investigations. The
first thing is a structural
survey by someone experienced
in such work, usually a surveyor.
Damp is the greatest single cause
of deterioration; settlement is
next. A services survey should
be made and a water test carried
out (if the water is not mains).
A valuation by a licensed valuer may be made, and this will
include the structural survey
and other investigations. A
visit to the local planning
office to check on any scheduled
development in the area comes next.

Financial Investigations. As to
rates, tithe redemptions etc. in
connection with the property.
Rateable value is the gross value
(annual rent possible) minus average annual cost of repairs,
insurance and other expenses.
Rates may change if alterations
are made.

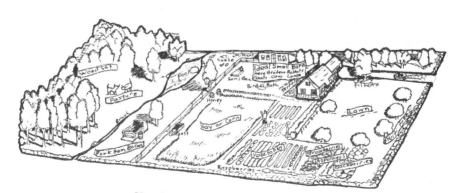

Here's a sketch of our homestead.

Legal investigations. Before contracts are signed, the purchasers' solicitor makes official search. Before the search certificates can become title deeds, the vendors' solicitor must send to the purchasers' solicitor, an abstract of title i.e. proof of ownership. When everything is in order, the solicitor will draw up a conveyance and in due course the completion takes place, after contracts are signed. The whole process takes a minimum of about 8 weeks.

Buying Land. In remote areas land can be very cheap, but it is difficult to live (legally) permanently on land which doesn't already have a dwelling on it. The best method of living on land unmolested by the authorities, would seem to be to have several pieces of land and stay for a part of the year on each in some type of moveable (i.e. temporary) dwelling. How well this works, will depend to a great extent on the relationship you have with the local people. Separate from the Local Authorities codes, rules and regulations, the country people have an unwritten lore and culture whose subtlety may take some time to appreciate. It is worth getting to know people of an area in which you are about to buy land and in which you may be unwelcome. It is also difficult to find bona fide small packets of cheap land for sale.

Choosing Land. Fertility is the first consideration. Avoid steep hillsides, Heather or Ling. Spurry, Samphire, Camophile and Tansy. Signs of good land are Thistles and Dock, Charlock, Bramble, Nettle, Ragwort and Yarrow. Presence of moles is a good sign; absence of rabbits is bad. Bracken or Larkspur indicates dry land. Dig several holes and examine depth and texture of the top soil in different parts of the land.
The second consideration is a good water supply of either a regularly running stream, or a reliable well.
The next thing is the lands position in relation to the prevailing winds i.e. whether it is sheltered or not.
Possible building material resources and site access must be studied. Take particular note of the rights of access, public footpath, easements etc.
Make use of a local solicitor who knows local land prices, and a land valuer if possible. The land value of agricultural land varies wildly, but may be approximated to the rent of 20 years lease less outgoings.

WILLIAM PENN BUYING THE LAND FROM THE IND
He would not take their land from them by force, but only after paying them a good value for it.

EXISTING STRUCTURES RECYCLED

It is often difficult to get planning permission for unusual types
of houses; but it is much easier to get permission for the conversion
of odd buildings to houses.

chapels
railway carriages
martello towers
boats
summer houses
army huts
factories
tim-mines
lighthouses
mills
poultry houses
forges
stables
shops
oasthouses

old barns
railway sheds
railway stations
railway tunnels (mushroom farm?)
mine shafts
backs of articulated vehicles
trees
pillboxes
bunkers
sectional buildings
eg nissen huts
garages
dove cotes
farm outhouses
forestry huts

Almost ANY unused structure will provide the basis for a goodtime house.

CONVERSION

A limit to what is enforceable?
Legal words make law
Terms of mutual agreement.
Consider ambiguity/flexibility of
ideas represented by words/terms
Discover meaning.

```
house............human habitation
                 (fitness for what)
permanent........temporary
farm.............animal pet..vermin
chair............comfort
window...........windscreen
encroachment.....trespass
home.............ownership
fixed abode......house
building..shelter..shed..marquee
lounge..workshop..greenhouse..hut
artist..hermit..monk..rabbit catcher
```

The legal system invariably supports
the cultural view of those in power.
Legalities such as planning permission may seem almost hopelessly res-
trictive in most areas and many
people are so put down by the im-
posed restrictions, that ideas of
really living somehow else are
quelled at conception. However, the
law is not comprehensively restric-
tive by any means. Twist. Its a
matter of being seen to be in a
suitable category. There are ways
in which you can live far out but
within THE LAW.

A temporary building does not
need planning permission in many
places. Can you dismantle it and
remove it within 24 hours?

A caravan without wheels is still
a moveable dwelling: but any
structure which is built into the
ground is a bye law building: and
a moveable building seems to be
anything which has been placed on
the soil and which could be removed therefrom without destruction
or displacement of its parts.

Bicycles are almost completely
unrestricted transport. No. tax,
insurance, driving licence, age
limits, tests or fuel.

"The great majority of crimes are
committed in respect of property
especially as regards to possession."
                Moriatys Police Law.

Life style seems to be limited to
a great extent by the words that
encompass the culture as it stands.
Stagnant categories.

A dwelling is "fit for human habitation" if it is reasonable
suitable for occupation with regard
to repairs, stability, freedom from
damp, internal arrangement, natural
lighting, ventilation, water supply,
drainage and sanitary conveniences,
facilities for preparation and
cooking of food and disposal of
waste water.

Turn of phrase in descriptions
submitted to authorities is all
important. A building described
as being supported by "old telegraph poles" was rejected by the
authorities. A re-application
was made with the same drawings
but the poles were described in
technical jargon e.g. 12" solid
pine pressure impregnated with
bituminous fluid." The applic-
ation was immediately passed!
Many planning applications are
passed or failed on the style of
the submission.

Trespass with no actual damage
done is a civil matter unlikely
to incur civil action as it is
so expensive, however if there
is actual damage, this is within
the jurisdiction of the magistrates.
Slight damage will suffice. Damage
does not include wild products of
the soil.

TENTS, HUTS, SHEDS and OTHER
TEMPORARY DWELLINGS.

Hogans are carefully sited so
as not to interfere with the
rights of others in respect of
grazing and water. For example
they are located "near water"
2 or 3 miles away rather than
adjacent, and timber is never
cut within one mile of someone
elses dwelling. The Hogan must
not intrude upon the landscape
of which it is part, but must
blend with it and be inconspi-
cuous. The care with which
the land is treated reflects
both an attitude to nature and
the importance of land and
landscape.

                   Navajo Indian Hogan
                   Shelter and Society
                       Paul Oliver

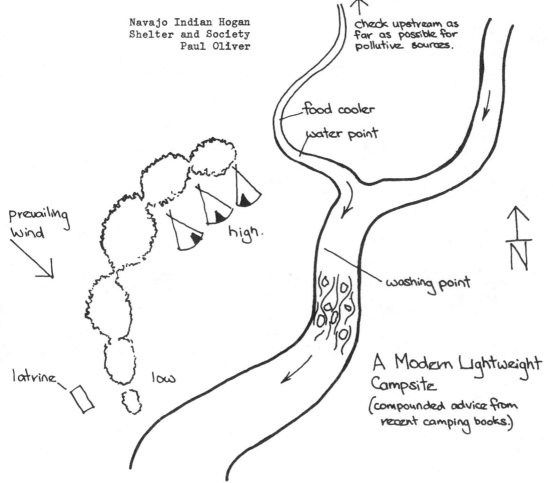

check upstream as
far as possible for
pollutive sources.

food cooler
water point

prevailing
wind

high.

washing point

latrine

low

A Modern Lightweight
Campsite
(compounded advice from
recent camping books.)

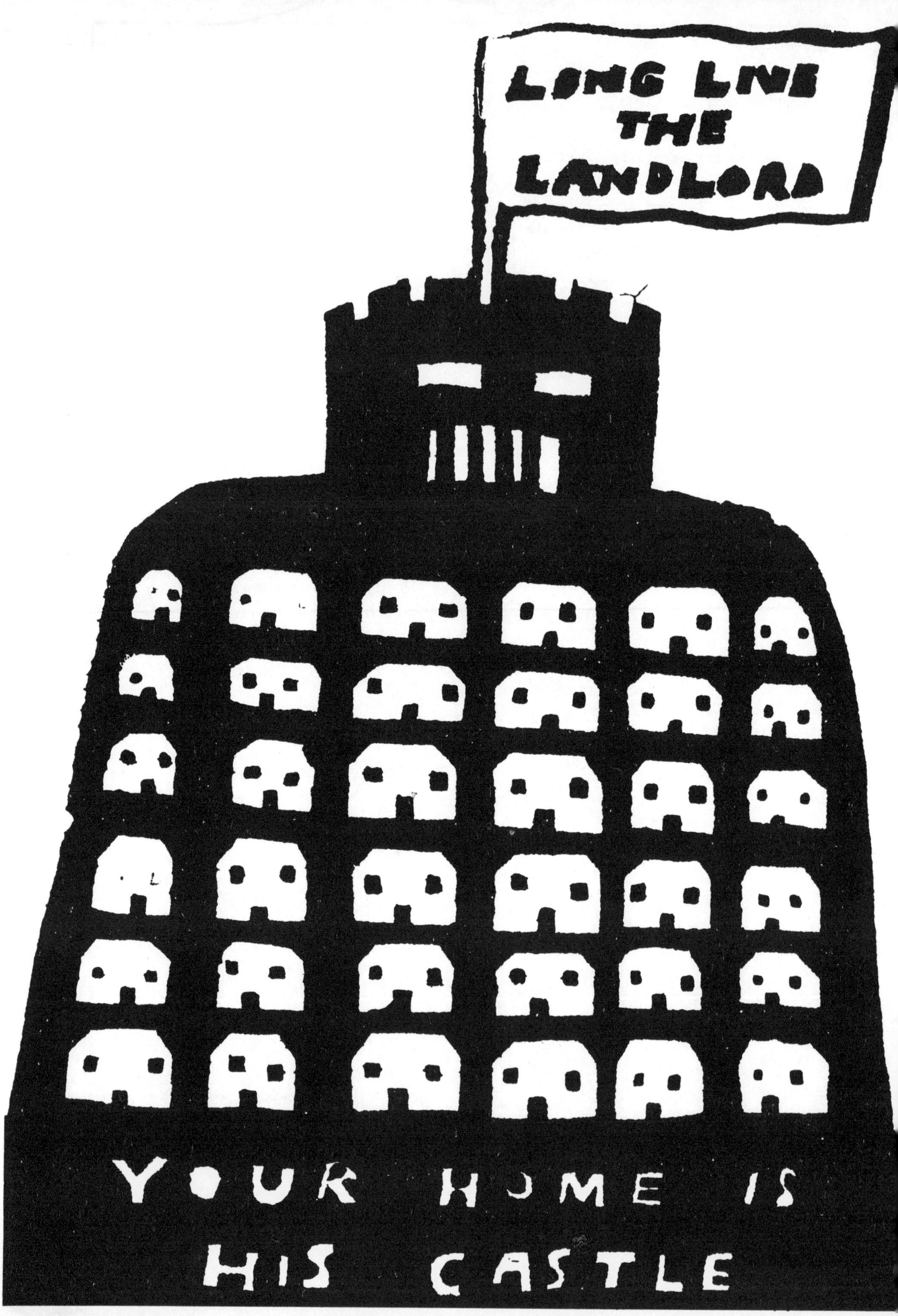
LONG LIVE THE LANDLORD
YOUR HOME IS HIS CASTLE

BIBLIOGRAPHY

General Introduction   (whole scrapbook)

ARCHITECTURAL DESIGN   (magazine) Standard Catalogue Co. 26 Bloomsbury Way W.C.1. 01 405 6325
ARTHUR D.R. Basic Resources for Survival   Survival - man and his environment   E.U.P. 1969
BAKER John   The Shell Book of Country Crafts   Shell 1968
BARR John editor   The Environmental Handbook action guide for U.K.   Ballantine 1971
BLACKSHAW Alan   Mountaineering from Hill walking to Alpine climbing   Penguin
CAGE John   Diary: How to improve the world. (you will only make matters worse) part three
                           A Great Bear Pamphlet. Something Else Press. 1967
CANADIAN WHOLE EARTH ALMANAC issues on shelter, food, industry. 341 Bloor St. West. Box. 6,
                                                         Toronto 181, Ontario. Portway
COBBET William. Cottage Economy
ESTYN EVANS E. Irish Folk Ways   R.K.P.
FIRST AID IN FACTORIES C.O.L. for Dept. of Employment & Productivity.
                             Health and Safety at Work booklet No.36.   H.M.S.O.
FIRST AID MANUAL   4, Grosvenor Crescent, London S.W.1.   Red Cross Society.
FOX Charles The Countryside and the Law   David & Charles 1971
FRANKENBERG Ronald   Communities in Britain   Pelican
GERAINT JENKINS J. Traditional Country Craftsmen   R.K.P. 1965
GREENBANK Anthony. The Book of Survival!   Wolfe. 1967
HUSSAIN Farooq. Living Underwater   Studio Vista
KNOWLES Joseph. Alone in the Wilderness   Longmans, Green & Co. 1914
NORTH E. Scott The Saga of the Cowboy   Jarrod
POCOCK Roger (compiler) The Frontiersmans Pocket-Book   John Murray. London. 1909
SPONS WORKSHOP RECEIPTS (4 vols.)   Spons. 1936
STREET FARMER (magazine)   63, Patshull Road, London. N.W.5. 01 485 3107
THE ADVANCED SCOUT STANDARD   Newnes. 1968
THE HOME LOVERS ENCYCLOPEDIA 1000 pp   The Amalgamated Press. 1934?
THE OXFORD HISTORY OF TECHNOLOGY (5 vols.)
THE VILLAGE TECHNOLOGY HANDBOOK 400 pages. $6.00   V.I.T.A. 1970
TRUEMAN A.E. Geology and Scenery in England and Wales   Pelican
USE AND CONSERVATION OF THE BIOSPHERE   U.N.E.S.C.O.
proceedings on the "Scientific Basis for the Rational Use and Conservation of the Biosphere"
conference. Paris. 4-13 Sept. 1968. (available through H.M.S.O.)
WALTER J.C. Copsford   Murray
WHOLE EARTH CATALOG. Last issue
ARCHITECTURAL DESIGN, MOTHER EARTH NEWS, NEW SCIENTIST are all good, informative magazines
buy them, and supply them.

GENERAL SOURCE ADDRESSES

BIT INFORMATION SERVICE 141, Westbourne Park Road.   01 229 8219

BLACKWELLS of Oxford. Good for U.S. books, also do useful bibliographies on currently
        available material e.g. farming.

B.L.U.P. pollution investigation 113, Warwick Avenue, London W.9.
(Biotechnic Land Use for Pleasure) 01 289 0286

Central Office of Information C.O.I. Hercules Road, Westminster Bridge Road, London S.E.1.

Colleges Most college people will give free advice, help, equipment, services, if
        approached diplomatically.

Co SIRA (country crafts in Britain) 35 Camp Road, Wimbledon Common, 01 946 5101

Forestry Commission 25 Saville Row, London W.1.

Hire Service Shops Head Office, Essex Road, London W.3. 992 0101
        For a limited period, hiring is cheaper than buying. You can hire
        almost anything.

H.M.S.O. Government bookshop, 49 High Holborn, London W.C.1.   928 6977

Intermediate Technology Development Group I.T.D.G. 9 King Street, Covent Garden, London W.C.2.
        01 TEMple bar 5211.

Kellys Business Directory Amazing.

Libraries are great energy storing systems. Unbelievably free. If you don't know anything
        try the librarian for your first lead. It will probably be your last.
        READERS GUIDES from the library Association, County Libraries Section. Useful
        general bibliographies e.g. Rural life, building, agriculture.
        (inter library loan will get almost any book, if you have full information on it).

London Ecology Bookshop 45 Lower Belgrave Street, London S.W.1. (catalogue on request.)

Meteorological Office London Weather Centre, 284, High Holborn, London W.C.1. 01 836 4311

National Council for Social Service (straight legal advice) 01 636 4066

National Trust 42 Queen Annes Gate, London S.W.1.

N.I.T.B. (development in N. Ireland) Royal Avenue, Belfast.

Peace Corps Technical Resources Division, Washington D.C. 20585

RELEASE 229 7753/727 7753 (emergency 603 8654)

The Highlands and Islands Development Board 6 Castle Wynd, Inverness.

United Nations Info. Centre & Library 14/15 Stratford Place, London W.1. 01 MAY 3816

V.I.T.A.   New York, U.S.A. 12308

Where to Buy Ltd. John Adam House, 17/19 John Adam Street, London W.C.2. 01 839 6171
        Lists published include: Building Construction. Agriculture & Horticulture.
        Electrical.

BIBLIOGRAPHY TWO

SHELTER

BIBLIOGRAPHY

GENERAL

ARONIN Jeffery Ellis. Climate and Architecture — Reinhold 1953

BATSFORD Harry & Charles FRY. The English Cottage — Batsford 1938

BRUNSKILL R.W. The Illustrated Handbook of Vernacular Architecture

CAMESASCA E. editor. History of the House — Collins 1971

C.I.R.I.a. Guide to Sources of Information. Construction Industry Research and
      Information Association. March 1970. 6 Storeys Gate, London S.W.1.

CRANFIELD S.W. and H.I. POTTER Houses for the Working Classes — Batsford 1900

DUNCAN R.F.H. Home-made Home — Faber 1947

HAGLUND Elsa. Housing and Home Improvement in the Carribean — F.A.O.1956

KERN Ken. The Owner Built Home Ken Kern Drafting 1961. Sierra Route, Oakhurst, CA93644

NAGY Moholy. Native Genius in Anonymous Architecture — Horizon NY 1959

OLIVER Paul. Shelter and Society Cresset Press. 63/- — Barrie & Rockliffe 1969

POLINGHORNE R.K. and M.I.R. Other Peoples Homes — Harrap 1945

RAPPAPORT Amos. Houseform and Culture — Prentice Hall 1967

RUDOFSK B. Architecture without Architects — Museum of Modern Art. N.Y. 1964

SALZMAN. Building in England down to 1540 — 1952

SPONS ARCHITECTS AND BUILDERS PRICEBOOK — yearly by Spons

TILLEY M.F. Housing and the Country Worker — Faber 1947

UNITED NATIONS. Methods for Establishing targets and Housing and Environmental Development-
                                  U.N. sales no.E. 68.1V.5. £1.00.

UNITED NATIONS. Improvement of slums and uncontrolled Settlements.
                                U.N. sales no. 71.1V.6. £1.96.

WOOD J.G. Strange Dwellings. habitations of animals — Longmans 1871

YOUNG Ernest. Homes Far Away. vols. 1 & 2 — G. Philip 1953

CLOTHING

CHRISTOPHER F.J. Hand-loom Weaving — Foyles handbook 1952

CLARKE Jane. editor. Manual of Shoemaking — Clarks 1966

JOHNSON Mary. Guide to Altering and Restyling Readymade Clothes — ARCO 1965

MINISTRY OF DEFENCE SPECIFICATION TC 167 Clogs (various) — reprinted 1948

THE PENGUIN KNITTING BOOK. 5/-

CAVES

BARING-GOULD S. Cliff Castles and Cave Dwellings of Europe — Seeley & Co. 1911

CULLINGFORD. British Caving — R.K.P. 1962

GREENBANK Robinson. Caving & Potholing. — Constable. 1964

JENKINS & WILLIAMS Caves of Wales and the Marshes — Dalesman

LOVELOCK James. Caving — Batsford 1969

MINISTRY OF POWER Support of Mine Workings. — H.M.S.O. 1966

MINISTRY OF PUBLIC BUILDING AND WORKS Advisory leaflets 51 & 52. Water-tight basements,
                        parts 1 & 2.

MORGAN REE D. Mines, Mills & Furnaces. an introduction to Industrial Archeology in Wales.
      (SBN 11 880083 3) — National Museum of Wales. £1.50. 1969

PEARSON H. Secret Tunnels in Surrey. Chelsea Speliological Society. — 1966

ROBINSON Don. Potholing and Caving. Know the Game Series. Educational Productions. — 1967

BIBLIOGRAPHY THREE

 OUT DOOR LIVING

ANGIER Bradford. How to stay alive in the woods.   Collier-Macmillan 1962
ANON. Outdoor Living.   Benjamin Edgington Ltd
BASILLIE & WESTWOOD. Mid-moor and Mountain.   Boy Scouts Ass. 1960
BROWER David. editor. The Sierra Club Wilderness Handbook.   Ballantine. U.S.A. 1971
COLBY & ANGIER. The art and science of Taking to the Woods.   Collier. U.S.A. 1971
H.M.S.O. Camping. Educational Pam. No. 58.   H.M.S.O. 65P 1971
HUNT Ben E. Indian Craft and Lore.   Hamlyn 1967
KEPHART Horace. Camping and Woodcraft.   Macmillan
JENNINGS F.L. Tramping with Tramps.   Hutchinson 1932
LAUBIN Reginald & Gladys. The Indian Tipi.   Univ. of Oklahoma Press. 1957
McLEOD W.M.A. Canvas-work for Seamen.   Brownson and Ferguson, Glasgow
WILLIAMS P.F. Camping and Hill Trekking.   Pelham 1969

 INFLATABLE

ANT FARM. Inflato Cookbook.   Ant Farm, 247 Gate 5 Road, Sausalito, CA 94965
PRICE & NEWBY. Research Report on Air Structures.   H.M.S.O. £4.25. 1971
PRICE & NEWBY. Air Structures - Bibliography. 38 Alfred Place, W.C.1.
                                                    Lightweight Enclosures Unit 1971
MINISTRY OF PUBLIC BUILDING & WORKS. Advisory Leaflet 74. Protective Screens and
                                      Enclosures.   H.M.S.O. 1969
SPICE H.R. Polythene Film in Horticulture.   Faber 1959

 MOBILE

A.A. LIBRARY. Low-cost, temporary, Mobile Housing.
               Bibliography of magazine articles.   Arch. Ass. Library. September 1971
ANON? The Caravan Manual.   Caravan Publications. (yearly)
ANON. Min. of Housing and Local Government. Welsh Office. Gypsies & Other Travellers.
                                                          H.M.S.O. £1.40 1967
COWLES F. Gypsy Caravan.   Hale. 1948
PETULENGRO Gypsy. A Romany Life.   Methuen. 1948
PHELAN J. We Travel the Roads.   Phoenix. 1949
  " "   Wagon Wheels.   Harrap. 1951
REEVE Dominic. No Place Like Home.
RODDIS Roland J. The Law Relating to Caravans. (rather out of date)   Shaw 1960
VESEY-FITZGERALD B. Gypsies in England.   Chapman & Hall 1940
YOORS D. The Gypsies.

 PAPER

        The Paper House Review. (article)   Arch. Design Mag. 10. 1970

GEODESICS

BAER Steve. _The Dome Cookbook._   Sl Lama Foundation U.S.A. Box 422 Corrales, New Mexico.

CRITCHLOW Keith. _Order in Space._   1969

CUNDY H.M. & ROLLET A.P. _Mathematical Models._   Oxford U.P. 1961

PACIFIC HIGH SCHOOL. _Domebook Two._ Pacific Domes, Box 219. Bolinas, CA 94924.

WOOD

ANDERSON L.O. _Low-cost Wood Homes for Rural America - a construction manual._
                                        U.S.gov. ₵1.00 1969
              from: Superintendent of Documents, U.S.gov. Printing Office, Washington
                                                                  DC 20402.

ANON? _The Thatchers Craft._   Rural Industries Bureau, 1961

ARNOLD James. _The Shell Book of Country Crafts._   John Baker 1968

BEDDALL J.L. _Hedges._   Faber 1950

BOULTON E.H.B. editor. _Timber Building for the Country._   Country Life 1939

FOREST PRODS. RESEARCH LAB. DEPT. of TRADE & INDUSTRY. _WoodBending Handbook._ H.M.S.O. 1972

FORESTRY COMMISSION. Forest Record No. 42. (71-12-42)
              Use of Home-Grown Softwood in House Construction.   H.M.S.O. 6P 1959

Note: for many other timber publications see H.M.S.O. Government Publications, Sectional
      List. Nos. 3 & 31.

HARRIS P.A. _A Handbook of Woodcutting._   H.M.S.O. 1946
            Forest Prods. Research Lab. Dept. of Trade & Industry.

LE SUEUR A.D.C. _Hedges, Shelterbelts and Screens._   Country Life 1951

McCLURE F.A. _Vamboo as a Building Material._   Peace Corps. 1969
            Peace Corps Tec. Resources Division. Washington DC 20525.

MINISTRY OF AGRICULTURE. _Round Timber from the Farm._   F.E.F.42. (25P.)
                         Shelter-belts for Farmland   F.E.F.15. (28P.)
                         Temporary Buildings of Pole Construction. F.E.F.45. (5P.)

RABORN J.M. _Shelterbelts and Windbreaks._   Faber 1965

SINCLAIR C. _The Thatched Houses of the Old Highlands._   Oliver and Boyd 1953

STOWE E.J. _Thatching Rick and Barn._   Landsmans Library 1957

WESLAGER C.A. _The Log Cabin in America._ Rutgers Univ Press New Brunswick, New Jersey 1969

EARTH

BRITISH STANDARDS INSTITUTE. B.S. 1377. _Methods of Testing Soils for Civil_
                                        Engineering Purposes.   London 1961
                            B.S. 1924. _Methods of Test for Stabilised Soil_ London 1957

BUILDING RESEARCH STATION? _Building in Cob and Pise de Terre._   H.M.S.O. 1922
                           Building Research Special Report No 5. out of print.
                           Tropical Building Studies. A.5.
                           Soil Stabilisation: A Review of Principles and Practice
                                        (47.215-5) 25P H.M.S.O. 1963

CODE OF PRACTICE 111. _Structural Recommendations for Loadbearing Walls._ London 1948

COOLING L.F. _Possibilities Presented by Cement Stabilised Soil._   H.M.S.O. 1939
            Building Research Station Note No. T.C. 1003.

DEPT. OF ECONOMIC & SOCIAL AFFAIRS. _Soil-cement - Its Use in Building._
                                United Nations. sales no. 64.1V.6. 57½P 1964

    "   "   "   "   _A Manual of Stabilised Soil Construction for Housing._
                                United Nations. sales no. 58.11.h4.

BIBLIOGRAPHY FIVE

EARTH

JAGGARD W.R. Experimental Cottages. Dept. of Scientific and Industrial Research
out of print H.M.S.O. 1921

MIDDLETON G.F. Build Your Own House of Earth.   Angus & Robertson 1953

MINISTRY OF AGRICULTURE. F.E.F.12. Roads of Local Materials 9P
                          F.E.F.19. Soil-cement Roads 9P

MINISTRY OF TRANSPORT. Road Research Lab. Papers. Technical Papers.
        17. The Compaction of Soil. A study of the Performance of Plant.
            F.H.P. WILLIAMS & D.J. MacLEAN.   H.M.S.O. 25P 1950
        13. Further Studies in the Compaction of Soil and the Performance
            of Compaction Plant. W.A.LEWIS   H.M.S.O. 25P 1954
        57. Soils and other Roadmaking Materials in Nigeria
            K.E. CLARE & P.J. BEAVAN.   H.M.S.O. 25P
        61. The Effect of Soil Organic Matter on the Setting of
            Soil-Cement Mixtures. P.T. SHERWOOD   out of print H.M.S.O 1962
        64. Investigations to assess the Potentialities of Lime for Soil
            Stabilisation in the U.K. M.J. DUMBLETON   H.M.S.O. 25P 1962
        Road Notes.
        15. Specification for the Construction of Housing Estate Roads
            Using Soil-cement.   H.M.S.O. 10P 1953

NEUBAUER L.W. Adobe Construction Methods   1964
        Agricultural Publications, 207 University Hall, Univ. of California,
        Berkeley, CA 94720.

THOMAS D.W. Small-scale Manufacture of Burned Building Bricks.   V.I.T.A.

V.I.T.A. Making Building Blocks with the CINVA Ram. A supervisors Manual   V.I.T.A. 1966

U.S. DEPT. OF COMMERCE. Handbook for Building Homes of Earth.   No. PB179 327
        from: U.S. Dept. of Commerce. Clearinghouse for Federal
        Scientific and Tech. Information. Springfield. V.A. 22151.

WILLIAMS-ELLIS C & EASTWICKFIELD J & E. Building in Cob, Pise and Stabilised Earth.
                                  Country Life second edition 1947

 STONE

BENFIELD E. Purbeck Shop: A Stoneworkers Story of Stone.   E.U.P. 1940

HOWE J.A. Geology of Building Stones.   Arnold 1910

MacDONALD. editor. Stephens Book of the Farm. (dry Stone Walling.)   1908

MITCHELL. Building Construction. (Stone Masonary.)   1902

NICHOLS. J.B. Introduction to Masonary.   E.U.P. 1936

RAINSFORD-HANNAY. Dry Stone Walling.   Faber 1957

WARLAND E.G. Constructional Masonary.   Pitman 1947
              Modern Practical Masonary. (second edition.)   Pitman 1953

WARNES. A.R. Building Stones.   Benn

 CONCRETE

HENDERSON F. Build Your Own Farm Buildings.   Farming Press 1966

LAKEMAN A. Concrete Houses and Small Garages.   Concrete Publ. 1949

PROPERTY

CONSUMERS ASSOCIATION. The legal side of buying a house.   1971
                        Extending your house   1971

DALTON CLIFFORD H & ENTHOVEN R.E. New Homes from Old Buildings.   Country Life 1954

DEPT. OF ENVIRONMENT & C.O.I. Money to Modernise Your Home   H.M.S.O. 1970
                               Disused Railways of England & Wales.   £1 H.M.S.O. 1970
                               (SBN 11 700489 8)
                               Crofter Commission Report for 1969. (SBN 11 490 414 6)
                                                                          H.M.S.O. 30P

DIETZ A.G.H. Dwelling House Construction.   Macmillan 1954

EVANS ASS. Complete Home Improvement Handbook.   McGraw Hill 1957

JOHNSTONE B.K. Building or Buying a House.   McGraw Hill 1945

MARTIN Stuart. Build your Own House.   Stanley Paul 1969

MINISTRY OF HOUSING AND LOCAL GOVERNMENT & C.O.I.
        House Improvements and Rents. (a guide for landlords and tenants)   H.M.S.O. 1970

RODGERS T.S. Plan Your House To Suit Yourself.   Scribner 1950

SHEA Charles. The Times Guide to Buying A House.   Times 1970

VICKERS L.E. Buying A House.   Penguin 1970

Note: The Estates Gazette (magazine) contains a comprehensive listing of
       specialist Estate Agents.

MISCELLANEOUS

ARCH. Research Lab. Architectural Research on the Structural Potential of Foam
                     Plastics for Housing in Underdeveloped Areas.   S5 1966
                        from: Publications distribution Service, University of
                              Michigan. 615 East Univ. AnnArbor, Michigan 48106

CHERNER N. Fabricating Houses from component parts: How to build a house
            for $6,000.   Reinhold U.S.A. 1957

C.O.I. for DEPT. OF EMPLOYMENT AND PRODUCTIVITY. Health and Safety at Work,
           Booklet 6E.
           Safety in Construction Work: Demolitions.   H.M.S.O. 1969

GIBSON Charles E. Knots and Splices.   Arco Mayflower handybook 1969

HOBBS E.W. Do Your Own House-repairs at low-cost.   Flousham 1953

HORNELL J. British Coracles and Irish Curraghs.   1938

MINISTRY OF PUBLIC BUILDING AND WORKS. Advisory Leaflets, including:
                            77. Adhesives used in building (SBN 11670237 0)
                            79. Vapour Barriers. (SBN 11 670254 0)
Note: for others see Gov. Publications Section List No.61.

MINISTRY OF AGRICULTURE. Minimum Standards for Glasshouse Construction.
                         Loading. STL106 free
                         Plastic Structures frr Agricultural & Horticultural Use. STL86 free
                         Mobile Greenhouse. AT465 free.

OTTO Frei. Tensile Structure. Vols. 1 and 2

PYCRAFT W.P. Camouflage in Nature.   Hutchinson 1925

U.S. ARMY. Camouflage. Basic Principles and Field Camouflage. FM 5 20.
           Dept. of the Army. Washington DC Jan. 1959.

WITTMANN Konrad. F. Industrial Camouflage Manual.   Reinhold 1942

BIBLIOGRAPHY SEVEN